# SALT

## IS ESSENTIAL

Food needs salt. The quantity is a matter of personal taste but some presence is essential: little is more disappointing from the eating perspective than a dish that looks fabulous and tastes of very little. It shows the cook's priorities are all wrong, that too much television cookery has been watched and not enough tasting and enjoyment indulged in. A little greediness is a great advantage.

Villainous quantities of hidden salts are a feature of industrialised food production, not home cooking, and not what we need worry over in our own kitchens or in any recipe here. A small hit of something salty, an anchovy or an olive perhaps, can lift a pedestrian combination of ingredients to a higher level, whereas too much scattered like a conjurer over a cauldron will make for a difficult dining experience.

# SALT

## IS ESSENTIAL

### AND OTHER THINGS I HAVE LEARNED
### FROM 50 YEARS AT THE STOVE

## SHAUN HILL

Photography by Tamin Jones

KYLE BOOKS

# CONTENTS

# 1

## CREATIVE THINKING

### IS A BAD IDEA IF YOU KNOW NOTHING

First stop for those seeking help and inspiration will be a recipe book. Cookery books come in two guises: manuals for those about to make things, and entertainment of a vaguely food and travel nature for those who are not. The constant between the two is the recipe. If the recipes are important to you as anything other than an appetising guideline then a book suited to your experience is called for.

Catering colleges use a textbook called *Practical Cookery* by Ceserani and Kinton that contains formulas that will work but not inspire. The presence of a college lecturer to explain why there are lumps in the white sauce or why the minestrone is tasteless is taken for granted – the objective is to build up experience of making basic preparations as swiftly as possible, ready for adaptation to the tastes and needs of whoever turns out to be employer.

> Confidence comes with experience and the understanding of what is central to a dish and what is peripheral.

At home, the best bet is to start with books that assume no practical experience on the reader's part, like those by Delia Smith. Carefully followed, every recipe will produce what it promises and in the fullness of time some understanding of why it all happens may dawn so that you can cook without help and with the expectation of success. In practice, most real, hands-on cookery involves continuous assessment of how ingredients look and feel at every stage. Confidence comes with experience and the understanding of what is central to a dish and what is peripheral. Until this point, all cooking is in effect carried out blindfold and the pitfalls increase with the complexity of the dish being attempted.

Writers like Jane Grigson assume some experience as well as an interest in food as produce not just ingredient. Cooking times, if any, will be vague because in reality that is what they are. To say that a rack of lamb may take 20 minutes at 200°C may well be true in spring when smaller new season lamb is on offer, when you are boiling new potatoes as accompaniment and have remembered to preheat the oven, but not in late autumn when the joints will be larger and denser from older animals – or even different breeds – and when the oven heat will be used to roast potatoes and parsnips at the same time. Neither do exact weights necessarily guarantee success. A kilo of beef fillet will vary in cooking time according to its thickness, whether it is taken from the head or tail end. The answer is to persevere because after a surprisingly short time, if you use brain, taste and touch all will be well. And you will be a better cook rather than just more widely read.

Then there are the books known as aspirational. Travel books where an image of the Mediterranean sun setting over gnarled old peasant ladies sits opposite recipes that call for ingredients available in only three villages in Tuscany, or chefs' books that are largely geared as a souvenir for those who have just eaten in their restaurant. All are or can be a good read and set the frame of mind that makes you want to cook better. However, it is as unwise to attempt Gordon Ramsay's or Raymond Blanc's signature dishes at an early stage in your cooking career, as it is to rewire the house or rebuild your car, with similar inexperience and just a diagram to follow.

Here are my tips:

- Read the recipe from start to finish before you weigh out the ingredients. Don't make substitutions or change anything the first time you make the dish.

- Check that your own equipment corresponds more or less with that indicated in the recipe. A different shaped cake tin for instance, broader or deeper, will affect the cooking time. With chefs' recipes, be aware that the recipes may not have been tested on domestic equipment. A chicken popped into my commercial oven will start to cook immediately, whereas the same bird placed in a domestic oven will lower the overall temperature for a while. Similarly, the shelf height selected will have an effect.

- If there is a photograph of the finished dish, check it against the ingredients you have in front of you. Should there be obvious discrepancies, maybe garnishes and flourishes not mentioned in the text, then disregard it as a guide completely. It will have been made to suit someone's visual aesthetic rather than to demonstrate what you will finish up with.

- Generally, the more often you make a dish the easier it gets because you will remember how the ingredients behaved together from the time before. It's not a great idea to attempt something new and complex when you are trying to impress guests at a special dinner party.

- Most important, remember that food must taste good, not just look good. The level of seasoning, with salt or whatever, is crucial to the eventual success of the dish. Soup that is served by the bowlful will need less strength than a tablespoon of sauce which may be required to enliven a piece of meat or fish ten times its volume. In the same way, a thick sauce – like hollandaise or béchamel – which will cling to the food it partners needs to pack slightly less punch than a thin one, say a Thai dipping sauce, which delivers only a thin film across each morsel.

It is as unwise to attempt Gordon Ramsay's or Raymond Blanc's signature dishes at an early stage in your cooking career, as it is to rewire the house or rebuild your car, with similar inexperience and just a diagram to follow.

# RESTAURANT DISHES ARE DIFFERENT

Restaurant dishes are different from those made at home. Not better, or worse, but different. Chefs spend all day making their prep, or *mise en place*, the stocks and dressing, the little pots of chopped herbs and shallots, skinned diced tomatoes and such like. Whether it's one o'clock in the afternoon or eight in the evening, most restaurants offer a choice of dishes, with a table of four ordering four different starters, main courses and puds, and of course many other tables will be simultaneously doing likewise. No food will have been precooked, so catering for everyone at once works because the piece of meat or fish can be cooked fairly swiftly and the garnishes and sauces that make it interesting

## Complex dishes for the professional chef are a doddle.

are assembled quickly from all those little jars and pots of prepared stuff. Something like a whole roast duck, which takes an hour and a half, doesn't work unless it is ready cooked then reheated – a poor substitute for what is better cooked at home. But complex dishes for the professional chef are a doddle.

The system perfected by the great French chef Escoffier for restaurant meals cleverly adapted traditional flavour combinations to the demands of an à la carte restaurant kitchen. The long, slow-cooked notes of a cassoulet or an osso bucco stew were replicated by roasting then simmering bones and trimmings for stocks and sauces, all of which could be usefully done in advance, then a piece of prime meat, maybe a loin or fillet, was quickly cooked and whatever herb and wine combination was in the original dish transferred to the sauce. The trade-off between cooking something rare or until it is well done is one of texture; longer cooking means more flavour but worse texture, so this method could deliver the best of both worlds. In theory at least.

The same system operates today but slanted towards modern taste. Advances in technology have also had an impact. Food processors can chop and blend things in seconds that a generation ago would have needed advanced knife skills and taken much time. Liquidisers will blend oils into sauces, and purée soups that would have been laborious in a traditional kitchen.

That's not to say that there aren't some restaurant dishes that are entirely suitable for a home cook and merit a revisit, so here are some raves from the restaurant grave for you.

# SOLE VÉRONIQUE

The classic French repertoire transformed a very few base sauces into an alarming diversity of menu items and gave the opportunity for huge menus and the largely bogus impression of great choice. Two of the standard bases, chicken and fish veloutés, all but disappeared when the ancien régime of Escoffier-style dishes and the restaurants that served them made way for a more democratic style of eating. Memories of hefty grub, sauces that slowly slid like molten lava, overcoming everything in their path, no longer fitted the bill. But they had their moments.

Fish velouté was made by whisking a strongly flavoured fish stock onto a roux of lightly cooked butter and flour in much the same way as any white sauce. The roux would slowly change from sludge into silky sauce as the hot stock was added and the slow simmering gradually, but thoroughly, cooked the flour.

The garnish would decide the name of the dish, thus a few spears of white asparagus on your poached sole fillets would be 'Argenteuil', whereas green asparagus would be described as 'à la princesse'. 'Joinville' signified shallots and parsley and any named white wine from Champagne to Chablis meant nasty cooking wine.

Best was sole Véronique. This came with peeled green grapes. The warm fish velouté would be slackened with some of the sole's poaching liquor, then egg yolk and a little whipped cream folded into the sauce. The sauce was spooned over the sole and grapes, then flashed under a red-hot salamander – the kitchen's overhead grill and toaster – for the sauce to brown like a Welsh rarebit. The grapes gave lift and balance to the creamy sauce without ever upstaging the subtlety of the poached fish. It tasted delightful and the punters could pronounce it.

Véronique? The dish was created by Escoffier in 1903 and named after a comic opera by André Messager that was being staged in London at the time.

# TOURNEDOS ROSSINI

Another operatic flourish, in which a combination of fillet steak, goose liver and Madeira sauce works perfectly. The classic dish also sported a slice of black truffle to round things off. This looked pretty but was largely wasted, flavour-wise, in the sweetish sauce.

A tournedos is a stovepipe-shaped cut from the middle of the fillet, designed to be served quite rare and shaped to provide height to the finished dish. The cooked meat would be placed on a round of toasted white bread, partly to soak up any meat juices, partly to make it look more impressive. A piece of cooked foie gras and a slice of black truffle went on top, then Madeira sauce would be spooned over the entire proceedings. I have used this recipe idea for both venison and pigeon and it works well with both.

Madeira sauce was easily assembled by reducing some Madeira wine in a pan, then stirring in what is known as demi glace (meaning half glaze) sauce. If the sauce was not thick or smooth enough, a knob of unsalted butter slowly stirred in as the sauce heated would put things right.

The key to the dish is the demi glace sauce base, and this is the awkward and time-consuming aspect. If you want to try your hand at home, make plenty because it freezes well and can be used, indeed was intended to be used, as the base for lots of different sauces. This is how it's made.

# DEMI GLACE SAUCE

First make a veal stock. Buy 3kg of veal bones and roast them. Transfer the browned bones into a large pot with about a kilo of washed and roughly chopped aromatic vegetables – onion, carrot, celery and leek. Add 5 litres of cold water and bring to the boil. Skim away any foam, then simmer the stock for about 8 hours, topping up the liquid as needed. You should end with about 3 litres of well-flavoured stock. Strain this into another large pot.

Wash out the original pot, then place back on the stove along with the strained stock. Fry, in batches, another kilo of washed and chopped aromatics, a couple of cloves of garlic and a kilo of diced beef shin. Add 2 tablespoons of plain flour to the frying veg and meat, then 2 tablespoons of tomato paste. Pour on half a bottle of cheap red wine, then stir this mixture into the stock. Bring to the boil, then simmer for 3–4 hours. Strain the liquor, which by this time is known as sauce espagnole, into a jug, then wash the pot once more. Return the sauce to the pot, bring to the boil, then simmer until about 2 litres of sauce is left. Voilà, demi glace.

Cooks make this, or some version of it, regularly. Sometimes the flour is omitted and the sauce called 'jus'. Well made it is a magic ingredient in sauces. Badly made it will be like gravy powder.

# STEAK DIANE

The role of the waiter has changed even more than that of the chef. A skilled waiter could give a virtuoso performance that transformed mealtime into cabaret. The balance and agility of a man or woman who could carry five plates of food without dislodging a single pea or bean was almost awe inspiring. The etiquette of delivering food from the right and removing plates from the left, deftly clearing and crumbing down the table so that no leftovers or debris were there to accuse you of clumsy eating. These were the minimum skills for junior waiters.

More experienced waiters, the *chefs de rang*, or captains in the US, would have carving skills because most meat was sliced in front of the table, just as most fish was cooked on the bone, presented, then ceremoniously filleted on a small table, a *guéridon*, wheeled alongside. Meanwhile, commis waiters, the least experienced, heated slivers of vegetable on a lamp so that they were piping hot before being spooned, not fork and spooned, onto the plate. This is silver service, and, properly done, has real advantages in that the diner can decide how much veg, sauce, meat or whatever they actually want rather than have the chef decide for them. It is expensive in staffing terms though and technically skilled so the art has mostly died out.

The idea of flambé work – cooking something straightforward in front of the table – is fine. Sadly, the reality was always pretty grim, pancakes and bits of meringue set alight for no good reason other than to impress morons and solicit tips. Among the more popular dishes subjected to this treatment was steak Diane, and this tastes quite good without all the fuss.

You will need a minute steak per person, some chopped shallots, button mushrooms, flat-leaf parsley and Worcestershire sauce, then a little brandy for the fireworks and some cream and mustard with which to dowse it. The frying pan needs to be hot before adding a little oil or butter. Season, then fry the steak quickly on each side. Lift the steak onto a dish, then add a touch more oil and butter to fry the shallots and mushrooms. Set the whole thing alight with brandy, then add a spoonful of mustard, Worcestershire sauce and cream. Return the steak to the pan to soak up all this stuff then add a good spoonful of chopped parsley and serve. It actually tastes okay.

Let us not forget where, until recently, French restaurant staff, kitchen and front of house, came from. They were Italians, regularly making very little effort to cook French food. They liked their own better and who can blame them for preferring what they knew. Italian dishes like *pollo alla cacciatora* mutated into *poulet sauté chasseur* and veal dishes like *vitello piccata al marsala* were standard issue on most menus.

# THE NEXT EXCITING IDEA

The mid-seventies brought Nouvelle Cuisine. This is much maligned but was a huge step forward from the travesty of classic French cooking that was then commonplace. A group of France's top chefs, including Paul Bocuse and the Troisgros brothers, spearheaded the movement. The idea was that a fresher look at top ingredients, free from the constraints of a traditional repertoire, could reflect the skills and preference of the chef and dish up some genuine excitement for diners. So, it became important to know who was the chef, the real beginning of the chef as lynchpin of any restaurant.

Nouvelle Cuisine wasn't meant to be all about huge plates and tiny portions, or even about the chef as artist, swirling brightly coloured bands of vegetable purée all around the plate. Not my personal taste in artistry of course, much closer and often inferior to my grandchildren's colouring books.

The fad came and eventually went. Now we have the chef as forager, primeval hunter-gatherer type and of course there will be positive aspects left by this phase also when it moves along to make way for whatever comes next. Interestingly, one of the more influential recent movements was the idea of the chef as scientist. Molecular gastronomy was a phrase invented by Oxford physics professor and food enthusiast, the late Nicholas Kurti. He arranged a week-long biennial workshop in Erice, Sicily, part funded by the Italian government. This consisted of about twenty people, mostly physicists, but always with two or three chefs, and the idea was that each presented a paper on the aspect chosen and that there would a daily session of practical experiments.

I gave the keynote speech at one session on flavours and wrote another on the meaning of 'fresh' as a culinary term – more complex than you may think. Top chefs like Pierre Gagnaire and writers like Harold McGee were there. Of course it was fascinating and educational, but a week away from earning my living will always be an occasional, rather than regular, treat. Heston Blumenthal took the spot I vacated afterwards and it's a tribute to him that he used the knowledge and experiments to start a really big development in restaurant cookery while I returned to my small restaurant to cook much the same as I had before, only with a tad more understanding.

Of course the major change over all this period has been to shift from French-inspired dishes to Italian. There is something generous and domestic in the best sense about Italian cookery and it would seem that the bad cooks and greedy restaurateurs haven't been able to discredit it. Not yet at least.

> There is something generous and domestic in the best sense about Italian cookery.

In the early seventies I worked for the cookery writer and restaurateur, Robert Carrier. At the time, charcuterie was popular, terrines and pâtés the latest obsession, so after a couple of years I was promoted to terrine-maker in chief, with my own separate kitchen, commis chef and kitchen porter to make these things on a grand scale: terrines in pastry, wrapped in boneless duck or chicken carcasses or squeezed into the centre of a brioche loaf. This was my favourite and I occasionally have it on the menu now. I'm sure the recipe has mutated over the years but it still works well and is worth the effort. This sort of pâté will keep for a week and freeze for much longer without too much deterioration.

# Mr Carrier's pâté aux herbes

FOR 12

Not sure that there is any real difference between a pâté and a terrine, other than the spelling. A terrine is an ovenproof rectangular dish. It's generally used for cooking highly seasoned chopped or minced food designed to be served cold. Anything cooked in a terrine will be called a terrine, just as anything cooked in a casserole, tian or whatever will be designated likewise, be it fish, liver, brawn or even vegetables. Anyway, we always cooked Carrier's pâté aux herbes in a terrine, just as we often took liberties with the recipes he gave us. The system worked like this: if Mr Carrier didn't like what was made he announced that we – I – hadn't quite followed the recipe properly. He was an immensely charming man so rarely rude. The recipe would be altered until he was happy, then we all agreed that I had followed it properly this time.

50g butter

500g fresh spinach

200g chicken livers

500g minced pork

4 eggs

1 tablespoon gelatine powder

6 fat garlic cloves – *chopped*

1 tablespoon *grated* nutmeg

1 teaspoon cayenne

4 tablespoons *chopped* basil

8 tablespoons *chopped* flat-leaf parsley

1 tablespoon *chopped* chervil

1 tablespoon *chopped* tarragon

200ml double cream

Melt the butter in a pan, then add the spinach, having first washed, dried and destalked it. When cooked, drain and squeeze dry, then purée in a liquidiser.

Trim the livers of gristle and green bits, then fry until pink.

In a bowl or using an electric mixer with the paddle attachment mix the pork, eggs, gelatine, garlic and spices. Add the spinach, the chopped herbs and cream. Mix until uniformly dull green.

Stir in the chicken livers, ham, tongue, pancetta and pistachios.

Line a 30 x 15 x 7cm terrine – or whatever you have, a loaf tin or large ovenproof dish of any description – with streaky bacon or lardo. Fill the centre with the mixture.

Place the terrine in a roasting tin half filled with water. Bake at 170°C/fan 150°C/gas mark 3 for 30 minutes, then reduce the heat to 150°C/fan 130°C/gas mark 2 for a further 30–40 minutes. Test the doneness with a skewer or sharp knife. If the skewer inserted into the centre emerges clean and warm the pâté is done.

Lift the terrine from the roasting tin and leave to cool at least overnight.

Serve in slices with piccalilli, chutney or celeriac remoulade, plus plenty of hot toast.

100g *cubed* cooked ham 100g cooked and *cubed* ox tongue

100g *cubed* pancetta

50g *blanched* pistachios

Plenty of salt and freshly ground black pepper

Enough streaky bacon or lardo to wrap the terrine

The spinach that colours the dish green can produce a fair amount of liquid, also there are quite a few whole eggs involved, so in order to be certain that the terrine set firm enough to carve into thick slices a small amount of gelatine was added to the mix.

We used shoulder, but any reasonably cheap cut of good pork is fine, even the posh supermarket's top grade of pork mince will do the job.

With all such dishes, a lot of seasoning is called for. Subtle is a bad idea and is far too close to concepts like bland or dull for comfort — taste the mix, raw pork isn't the worry it may have been in the 1940s. Anything eaten cold needs to be stronger flavoured than anything served warm.

# Rack of lamb with persillade and gratin de Jabron

FOR 6

This was the Capital's most popular main course during my time there in the late 1970s. The recipe is straightforward for both parts of the dish. The initial menu for the place had been devised by a French chef, Pierre Gleize, who had a restaurant, La Bonne Etape, in the French Alps. The Jabron of the potato accompaniment is the name of the valley near his restaurant. Persillade is a stuffing, in this instance used to make a crust. It has variations that include chopped garlic or even lemon zest. There's plenty of garlic elsewhere in this dish, so no more needed here. The idea is that the persillade is pressed onto the racks of lamb as they rest after being roasted and that the juices from the meat combine with it before being crisped under a grill or in a hot oven. The potato gratin is one of my favourites and once the ingredients are prepared will require the same length of cooking and the same oven temperature as the lamb.

. . . . . . . . . . . . . . . . . . . . . . . . . . . . . . . . . . . . . . . . . . . . . . . . . . . . . . . .

1 pair of best ends of lamb – *prepared as racks*

A little oil *for cooking*

1 tablespoon Dijon mustard

### Gratin

1kg maincrop potatoes – *of a similar size if possible*

3 large garlic cloves

40g unsalted butter

300ml milk

300ml double cream

50g *grated* Gruyère or mature Cheddar

### Persillade

4 tablespoons each unsalted butter, fresh breadcrumbs and *chopped* flat-leaf parsley

1 small onion – *chopped*

Salt and freshly ground black pepper

First make the gratin. Gently simmer the potatoes in their skins, so that they cook right through without disintegrating. Drain, and when cool enough to handle, cut into large dice. Crush the garlic and add this and the butter to a wok or frying pan over a low heat. When the butter has just about melted stir it and the garlic together, then add the cooked potatoes. Season well with salt and black pepper, turning the potatoes so that they are lightly coated with the garlic butter. This need not be done with any extra heat. The idea is to coat the potatoes rather than fry them. At this point they can be kept for hours or even overnight in the fridge because they won't discolour. When you cook the meat, you can scoop the potatoes into a reasonably deep ovenproof dish and cover with the milk and cream. Sprinkle over the cheese or a mixture of these and Parmesan. At the Capital we bought all the offcuts of hard white cheese that Harrods Food Hall was willing to sell reasonably cheaply and grated those.

To make the persillade, warm the butter and onion together then, add the breadcrumbs and parsley. Season well with salt and black pepper. This too can be kept until needed.

Preheat the oven to 180°C/fan 160°C/gas mark 4. Season and sear the racks in a little oil on each side then roast in the oven until pink, depending on the size of the eye of the meat about 20 minutes. You can put the garlic-coated potatoes in the oven at the same time. Lift from the oven and brush with mustard. Pat the persillade onto the lamb then let it rest for 5 minutes. Crisp under a grill. The potatoes will take about 35 minutes so should have thickened and browned by this time.

# PREPARING A RACK OF LAMB

If you have a good butcher then he or she can do this for you. The problem with butchers and this type of joint is that their training is designed to achieve the most favourable cost per kilo, so the more bone and fat they can leave on the happier they will be.

A pair of best ends looks like a saddle. Use a sharp knife to cut down each side of the back bone. When you reach the corner, cut around it for an extra half inch along the rib bones. Pull the meat away, then use a chopper to separate each rack from the chine (backbone) so that you have also cut off the base bone of each cutlet but not lost any meat. You do this so that the irritating little bones at the base of each rib are lost and the meat can be sliced easily into cutlets once cooked.

Lift the entire flat of skin and fat upwards from each rack, then cut it away with a sharp knife, cutting almost towards the rib bones.

Lay the racks meat side down and chop away the top third of the line of bone. What's left is the eye of the meat held to the remainder of the ribs.

# Malfatti

FOR 4

The huge influence of Italian cookery has often concentrated on the starch element: pasta, rice, polenta or pizza base. These dumplings are overlooked. The name is unfortunate, malfatti sounds like something badly made, but they are both light and delicious.

. . . . . . . . . . . . . . . . . . . . . . . . . . . . . . . . . . . . . . . . . . . . . . . . . . . . . . . . . . . . . . . . .

4 tablespoons *chopped onion*

10g butter

115g spinach, *cleaned and any coarse stalks removed*

340g ricotta – *drained for 2 hours*

55g *grated* Parmesan

1 whole egg, plus 1 yolk

¼ teaspoon *grated nutmeg*

¼ teaspoon *grated lemon zest*

4 tablespoons 00 flour *plus extra for dusting*

Salt and freshly ground black pepper

### Sauce

900g fresh tomatoes – *roughly chopped*

100g unsalted butter

4 sprigs of basil

2 dashes of Tabasco sauce

Parmesan shavings – *to garnish*

Olive oil

Sweat the onion in the butter and cook until soft but not browned. Add the spinach and cook for another few minutes until it wilts. Season with salt and pepper, then drain in a colander until cool.

Chop the spinach and onion mix until fine. In a large bowl combine the ricotta, Parmesan, whole egg and yolk, nutmeg and lemon zest. Finally, add the spinach, then gently stir in the flour to form a stiff mixture.

Use two large spoons dipped in warm water to form round dumplings. Slide these onto a floured tray. They shouldn't touch each other. Refrigerate for 2 hours.

To make the sauce, heat the tomatoes in a saucepan, then thicken with the butter by stirring it in 5g at a time to make a sauce. Chop the basil leaves and stir these in also. Season with salt, pepper and Tabasco, then leave until needed.

Bring 4 litres of salted water to the boil. Slide in the malfatti. Once they rise to the surface, allow to simmer for 7 minutes. Lift out with a slotted spoon. Warm the sauce and place the malfatti on top. Garnish with Parmesan shavings and a drizzle of olive oil.

CREATIVE THINKING IS A BAD IDEA IF YOU KNOW NOTHING

# 2

## BREAKFAST ARRIVES
## TOO EARLY IN THE DAY

Breakfast is the first meal of the day. This may seem a little obvious but breakfast and supper are the only two eating opportunities upon which all agree, timing wise. In my childhood, dinner was generally held to be the meal eaten in the middle of the day and the final repast was called tea. This still holds true for a fair proportion of the British population, but can be confusing. Also, it simply will not do for those of us in the cooking trade who need to know, when asked for a table for dinner, what time is meant. So the rule is: first breakfast, then lunch, then dinner. If you like to call dinner supper, that's okay too, so long as nobody believes it is a more clever or classy term. Elevenses and afternoon tea can be slotted in for the greedy, and early-morning tea – at around six in the morning – would appear to be in steep decline with the death or decay of those old enough to have been conscripted in the army in the last world war.

> Those of us with a good social life or serious drink problem are not ready for devilled kidneys or kedgeree while negotiating the idea of being awake and requiring to function.

My view of breakfast is that it arrives far too early in the day. Those of us with a good social life or a serious drink problem are not ready for devilled kidneys or kedgeree while negotiating the idea of being awake and requiring to function. I have to assume that our European partners and traditional enemy from across the Channel came to terms with this fact early on as the 'continental' breakfast comprises very little apart from sweetened bread and coffee.

If we assume that normal folk will have been awake for a little while, maybe have read the papers or walked the dog, we can proceed with the business of breakfast with some genuine enthusiasm.

## BRUNCH

This gruesome word, a collision between breakfast and lunch, has been around for over a century. The meal described is, though, a fine idea if your schedule allows a sizeable break from whatever you do in the late morning rather than the customary lunchtime. Egg Benedict – muffin, ham, poached egg and hollandaise sauce or a dozen equally fine variations using maybe smoked salmon or grilled trout fillets in place of the ham – is what's centre stage. It's the egg dish's big moment – with filled omelettes and scrambled egg concoctions moving to main-course stardom.

Brunch became a famous institution in New Orleans where an accompanying jazz band is on the cards on a Sunday morning. At Brennan's, in Royal Street, breakfast/brunch starts at 9 o'clock and finishes around one. As well as standards like egg Benedict and oysters Rockefeller, those with serious appetites can tuck into steaks followed by flambéed bananas or bread pudding. All washed down with Bloody Mary, Bull Shot, Gin Fizz or Sazerac – a mixture of Bourbon and absinthe. Very fine.

Buffet style works as well for brunch as it does for breakfast generally and means there is a spot for tarts and quiche as well. It was traditional in England for the leisured classes to help themselves from a sideboard at breakfast time, rather than place an order and wait for dishes to appear, and buffet works very well in a hotel or restaurant setting also. Of course, no couple in their right minds are going to lay out a buffet for themselves alone, but with a house full of guests, or in my case children and grandchildren, a version of breakfast/brunch buffet still makes sense – a tray of sliced hams, mild cheese like Gouda or Appenzeller, fruit salad or juice, yogurt with bananas and wheatgerm or demerara sugar, some decent bread, boiled eggs and all the day's newspapers so that conversation is optional for those still not fully awake.

## BREAKFAST CEREALS AND PORRIDGE

Commercially manufactured cereals like Corn Flakes and Rice Krispies are easy and quick, vegetarian, fairly light and perceived to be healthy. Small wonder that they have achieved such popularity since Mr Kellogg came up with the corn flake process at the end of the nineteenth century.

At about the same time, Dr Bircher-Benner developed his muesli recipe to form the breakfast bit of a healthy regime at his clinic in Switzerland. Surprisingly, it took a long time to achieve any popularity. In the sixties it was sold only in specialist shops and was called Birchermuesli. Rolled oats are soaked rather than boiled and lots of fruit and nuts mixed in to make it all palatable. There are plenty of ready-mixed mueslis on the market. They all tend to be mean with the expensive ingredients like nuts and generous with the oats so the addition of a little more of what you fancy will do it good.

Large chunks of the global population eat some form of porridge first thing. Scotland's oatmeal boiled in water then finished with milk or cream may spring to mind, but the word describes any gruel-consistency dishes from Italian polenta and Indian dhal to Chinese rice congee. A lighthearted dismissive reference to Scotland's pride and joy in a treatise on ancient food once got me a ticking off in *The Scotsman* newspaper, so I must be careful to say that if patriotic Scots see porridge as emblematic of nationhood, then good luck and bon appétit.

# EGGS

Hen's eggs are generally what's on offer. Larger eggs have thinner shells so will absorb air more quickly. This means that although fresh, they are more likely to lose shape when cooked, and the yolks are fragile. A bantam's egg, in comparison, will sit proud on the frying pan a lot better at the same sell-by date. The size of egg depends on the age of the hen: the older the bird, the larger the egg.

Duck eggs are a bit larger, creamy and equally delicious but basically not much different. There is a short season in Britain for gulls eggs (from April onwards for five weeks), which are eaten hard boiled with celery salt. I like all boiled eggs, but find the prices asked for gulls eggs unappetising. Nice to take some revenge on the creatures that defecate on cars and heads across the country, however. Quails' eggs have a dinky, Lilliputian, quality that endears itself to professional chefs. Two minutes in boiling water for soft boiled, twice that for hard, and lovely to look at and eat if you have the patience.

*Scrambled eggs* – patience is the key. Melt a small knob of butter in a pan over a very low heat, then beat the eggs with salt and black pepper. Pour onto the butter and draw a wooden spoon carefully across the setting egg mix, back and forth until the eggs are cooked the way you want. The slower you scramble the eggs the better they are. If you want a particularly creamy result, then stir in a little cream or extra butter towards the end of cooking. The accompaniment to a breakfast egg dish like this is less important than the care with which the central ingredient is cooked. Scrambled eggs are fine with smoked salmon or prosciutto. Try not to add any raw cured fish or meat to the scrambled egg too early or it will cook into a dull version of its glorious raw self. Cooked smoked salmon is a silly idea of course and none of you would ever make it. The same holds good for prosciutto.

*Poached eggs* – ideally two pots of boiling water are called for, one acidulated with a little vinegar added, the second without vinegar but with salt. Crack the eggs into individual saucers or ramekins. When the acidulated water comes to the boil, turn down the heat and slip each egg into the water. Allow the eggs to poach for 2-3 minutes without returning the water to a fast boil. Lift the poached eggs with a slotted spoon into the salted simmering water for a few moments, then lift onto a serving plate. If you don't want to use two saucepans, then cook the eggs in salted acidulated water and pat dry after cooking. That's if you like the taste of vinegar on poached egg of course. Personally I don't.

*Fried eggs* – dangerous territory for advice because the method seems so simple. Americans have a more precise and useful vocabulary for fried eggs and my preference is for 'over easy' that is, not too cooked but without patches of raw egg white on top. This is achieved by either flipping the egg in the pan or putting it under a grill to set. Variations of this method, called 'oeufs en cocotte' or more prosaically 'baked eggs' involve greasing an ovenproof dish with butter or cream, cracking an egg into it and baking it until set. All egg dishes can be ponced up with herbs, mushrooms, slices of ham or, of course, truffles.

*Boiled eggs* – remember the simple things. The size and temperature of the eggs will affect the cooking time. Several eggs added to boiling water simultaneously will lower the water temperature, which will take longer to reboil. The eggs will continue to harden once out of the water. Four minutes for a medium-sized egg is perfect to produce a thickening but still runny yolk and a completely set white.

## OMELETTES

A clean, dry and hot frying pan is crucial. Heat a little oil – not butter – in the pan then beat the eggs, two or three as you prefer, with salt and black pepper. Slide the beaten egg plus a small knob of butter into the hot pan. Leave it alone for a second to set, then use your wrist to flick the mixture forward and back as if tossing a pancake, each time allowing a second for the egg to set. If you like a wettish (baveuse) omelette, fold the cooked egg mixture across and turn directly onto a warmed plate. If you prefer the omelette more set, less sloppy, then use a fork to briefly stir the egg mix in the frying pan before folding. A cold pan or constant annoyance of the cooking egg with a fork will produce creditable scrambled egg but inferior omelettes. The essentials are these: don't beat the eggs until the very last moment – I beat them over the heating pan and slide the mix straight in. This gives a full, pillowing and light texture, whereas a dish of long whisked egg will give a flat dull result. The pan should be hot. If you are adding cheese, then take care because the more cheese you use, the softer and less likely to set will be the result. If you are adding wet ingredients like tomato, then do so when the omelette is almost cooked.

# Lobster omelette Victoria

This will make a brunch or lunch that much more grand. It's reminiscent of the Savoy's famous omelette Arnold Bennett, which has smoked haddock as its main ingredient. It is certainly not a dish to be faced with just after waking and calls for a mixture of Cheddar cheese-flavoured white sauce and hollandaise.

FOR 4

...............................................................................................................

1 x 1kg lobster, *boiled and shelled*

50g unsalted butter

40g plain flour

400ml whole milk

50g *grated* Cheddar

1 teaspoon Dijon mustard

A few drops of Worcestershire sauce

8 eggs

6 tablespoons hollandaise sauce (see page 31)

Salt and freshly ground black pepper

Cut the lobster meat into large chunks and gently warm through in warm water or stock. Don't let the liquid approach boiling point or the meat will shrink and toughen.

Melt the butter in a large frying pan, then stir in the flour. Let this cook for a couple of minutes before adding the milk, one-third at a time, stirring each time until smooth. Season the sauce with salt and black pepper, then stir in the cheese, mustard and Worcester sauce. Of course, you can do this in advance and reheat if that suits you better.

Beat the eggs, two at a time, and make four omelettes; flat ones are better than folded.

Place the warm lobster on top.

Mix the hollandaise with the cheese sauce and spoon over each omelette.

Gratinate under the grill.

# Hollandaise sauce

ENOUGH FOR 6 EGGS BENEDICT

Traditionally, hollandaise is made by whisking egg yolks and a little water over a pan of hot water, then incorporating clarified butter and a reduction of shallots, peppercorns and vinegar as flavouring. My preference is for a light sauce, so I alter the proportions slightly, using much more white wine with the egg yolk, less butter and no reduction. If you have ready a saucepan of simmering water the whole business will take only a couple of minutes.

Hollandaise should be made fresh and kept only for about half an hour. Two reasons: the sauce will cool and turn into something less creamy and unctuous, more the texture of cheesecake than sauce; or, if kept warm, it will lose liquid through evaporation and this will eventually unbalance the emulsion between butter and other liquid, causing the sauce to split. Hollandaise, like its related sauce, beurre blanc, should be a pleasing balance between sharp and buttery rather than warm mayo or even just warm butter. Adventurous types will realise that you can add all sort of flavours to hollandaise, the best known is béarnaise sauce with tarragon and vinegar, but of course any herb that suits the occasion will do, also things like tomato passata, toasted nibbed almonds or reduced blood orange juice. Most of these variants will have grandiose names, sauce choron, sauce maltaise and so on, but the standard sauce will be what works best on top of a poached egg.

Egg Benedict is, of course, a tower of toasted muffin, ham and poached egg.

---

250g unsalted butter

3 egg yolks

70ml white wine

1 tablespoon lemon juice

4 dashes of Tabasco sauce

Salt

Melt the butter in a frying pan, then allow it to heat until it separates into brown clarified butter with a milky residue at the bottom, which serves no purpose and can be discarded.

Put the yolks and wine into a round-bottomed stainless steel bowl and bring a saucepan of water to the boil.

Set the egg and wine mixture over the simmering water and whisk until it thickens and cooks. The time taken will depend on how hot the water is.

Slowly whisk the clarified butter into this mixture, then whisk in the lemon juice, Tabasco and as much salt as you feel is needed.

Transfer the sauce to a heated jug – I fill a jug with the hot water just used, then pour it away, leaving a nicely warmed jug – until needed.

# Karjalan piirakka

MAKES 10

These rye pastry snacks come from Karelia, the province of Eastern Finland swallowed up by the Soviet Union after the Second World War. Finland took in a fair proportion of the population, and these savoury pasties are much loved in the region. They are small, flattish and moccasin-shaped rather than Cornish pasty-shaped. They can be made with either a rice or a potato filling and are served with coarsely chopped boiled egg that has been seasoned and stirred with butter. All nicest warm.

## Filling
100g short-grain rice

1 teaspoon salt

600ml whole milk

## Dough
15g unsalted butter

100g rye flour, plus extra for dusting

75g plain flour

½ teaspoon salt

25g butter

50ml whole milk

## To serve
6 boiled eggs

25g soft butter

Salt and freshly ground black pepper

Make the filling by boiling the rice for about 20 minutes in 300ml cold water and the salt until the water has almost all evaporated. Add the milk, then reduce the heat to a simmer. Cover and cook slowly for a further 15 minutes, by which time the rice should be tender. Stir regularly because rice pudding can easily stick and burn. Leave to cool.

Make the dough. Melt the butter in a pan and pour it into a large bowl. Mix in the flours and salt, then 100ml cold water. Mix into a dough, knead a couple of times to be sure everything is evenly mixed, then divide into 10 small balls. Roll out each ball on a floured surface so that you have 12cm rounds. These will harden in the air quite quickly, so if you are not ready to complete the dish sprinkle with a little rye flour and stack on top of each other.

Place a tablespoonful of the cooked rice into the centre of each round. Turn the edges of the dough back towards the middle so that they don't quite cover the filling – remember it's a moccasin look you want. Crimp these edges and then place the pasties on a baking tray. Bake at 200°C/ fan 180°C/gas mark 6 for 10–15 minutes.

Melt the 25g butter and stir in the milk. Brush this over the cooked pasties, cover with a clean napkin or cloth to soften.

Chop the boiled eggs fairly coarsely, then stir in the butter, salt and black pepper. Serve the chopped egg mix with the pasties – these are best warm so a brief return to the oven is called for.

# FISHCAKES

It's hardly worth dignifying fishcakes with a recipe. Make a dry, well-seasoned potato mash, then make the same volume of poached fish, broken into flakes. Smoked fish – haddock or the very fine lightly smoked salmon fillets now available – is best, add an egg yolk, then form into patties for shallow frying. Supermarkets, and the well-known high street knicker and underpants shops, used to make perfectly decent fishcakes that would save you even this minor bother. But of course, the creeping demands of profit margin have decreed a steadily smaller ratio of fish to spud.

There is another style of fishcake, usually crabmeat, held together with mayonnaise rather than mashed potato. These are generally tiny, fritter-like jobs, which are well spiced and really suit a starter salad more than the comfort-seeking demands of early morning.

# Kedgeree

FOR 6

This is a great breakfast dish, soothing and gently spicy. Americans have little connection with, or nostalgia for, India so it has never featured in their repertoire of brunch options despite being an ideal candidate. This recipe is complex rather than simple, but you can make it in advance because it reheats well. The smoked haddock called for is the Finnan, cold smoked, rather than Arbroath, the hot-smoked variety. Smoked eel makes excellent kedgeree, but raises the cost dramatically.

Kedgeree leftovers, if not overcooked, make an interesting version of arancini – cold risotto which is formed into balls, breadcrumbed, then deep fried. Mould the kedgeree into small balls, egg and breadcrumb, then deep fry. Serve with a teaspoon of curried mayonnaise. Very fine with cocktails later in the day.

25g green lentils

1 tablespoon vegetable oil

1 tablespoon *chopped* fresh ginger

1 garlic clove – *crushed*

1 large onion – *chopped*

½ teaspoon each ground cumin and coriander

2 teaspoons curry paste or powder

1 tablespoon lemon juice

2 smoked haddock fillets

300ml whole milk

30g butter

20g plain flour

3 boiled eggs, *shelled and roughly chopped*

150g raw rice – *cooked pilaf or plain boiled*

2 tablespoons *coarsely chopped* flat-leaf parsley

1 tablespoon *coarsely chopped* coriander leaves

Most small pulses, like green or brown lentils, don't really need prolonged soaking. The timing will vary according to the dryness of the lentils, but 30 minutes in cold water is a good guideline. Drain, then simmer in unsalted water until tender. Timing will depend on how old and dry the pulses might be – think 15 minutes but be prepared for double. The idea is to produce a gently spiced dhal that will flavour the kedgeree without overpowering the fish.

Heat the oil and fry the ginger, garlic and onion until starting to colour, reduce the heat and stir in the spices and curry paste. Stir in the cooked lentils, then add enough cold water to just cover. Simmer for 30 minutes, replacing the liquid as it evaporates, then blend in a liquidiser, adding salt and the lemon juice.

Cut the smoked haddock fillets into manageable pieces and poach gently in the milk, covering the pan with a lid.

Melt the butter in a separate pan, then stir in the flour to make a roux. Let this cook for 1 minute then stir in a couple of tablespoons of the poaching liquor. When this has thickened pour in the remaining cooking liquor and stir to the boil. You should have a thin white sauce.

Combine this sauce with the spiced lentil purée, haddock, boiled eggs and cooked rice. Adjust the consistency if necessary by adding more milk or butter – you are looking for a soft but not sloppy porridge. Finally, add the coriander and parsley.

# Baked beans

ENOUGH FOR 10-20

Open a tin or bake your own? Depends, of course, on your time and taste buds. However, you won't need any advice from me for the first option, so best to concentrate on the second.

Commercial brands are variations on Boston baked beans, which are quite sweet. In truth, most of these are okay by tinned food standards, if a touch innocuous. This recipe using smoked bacon, paprika and chilli will produce a rather more potent product and will partner duck, meatballs or pork as well as sit on toast with a sausage at breakfast time. No sensible person is going to spend 4–5 hours cooking a side dish for breakfast, so make a large batch – it keeps well and can be frozen.

1kg haricot beans

50g lard or goose fat

2 medium onions – *chopped*

6 fat garlic cloves – *chopped*

1 tablespoon smoked paprika – *Spanish is very good, otherwise regular*

400g tin chopped tomatoes – *I'm partial to the Cirio brand but any will do*

2 tablespoons Dijon mustard

300g fatty smoked bacon – *in one piece*

100g brown sugar

2 tablespoons molasses or treacle

Worcestershire sauce

Salt

Soak the beans overnight in cold unsalted water. Drain, then bring to the boil in fresh unsalted water. Simmer for 15 minutes, then drain.

Preheat the oven to 150°C/fan 130°C/gas mark 2. Heat the lard in a large, heavy-bottomed casserole and fry the onions and garlic until starting to colour.

Add the remaining ingredients (minus the Worcestershire sauce and salt) and just enough water to keep the beans moist – about 500ml should do it. Cover and bake for 5 hours. At the end of each hour, check the beans, top up the water and give a good stir. When the beans are done, stir in the Worcestershire sauce and salt.

# BACON AND SAUSAGES

Bacon is a reasonably straightforward ingredient. Back bacon is the cured, and maybe smoked, pork loin, and streaky is belly. The differences come from the quality and breed of pig used, and of course the taste and skill of the butcher. There has been a resurgence in rare-breed, flavoursome pig rearing, which is good news, but a decline in the number of butchers capable of curing the pork, which is less fine. Not sure why this should be.

Sausages need a fair amount of good-quality fat or they will be dry and dull. Worthy sausagemakers, trumpeting 100 per cent meat, regularly make poor specimens reeking of dried herbs.

We are talking of the traditional British sausage here of course rather than any German, Polish or French variety and most bockwurst and Frankfurter types suit mashed potato and beer rather than breakfast in any case. Of course, ham sausages and charcuterie make a glorious start to the day alongside some cheese, a non frightening type like Appenzell or Gouda, and warm bread.

# Black pudding

MAKES 12 SERVINGS

There are several styles of black pudding, depending on what, if any, cereal is used to thicken the result. Usual alternatives are rice, as in Spanish morcilla; fresh breadcrumbs, as in France; or oatmeal, as in the British version. Each will affect the final result slightly differently.

My version has the pork blended into the pudding mix rather than dotted about in chunks and is flavoured with a little roasted apple. It differs mainly in that I don't fill sausage casings with the mix (which is a messy and pointless exercise), rather I bake it in a deep tray, then cut the result into squares for frying or grilling when needed.

Fresh pig's blood is difficult to obtain, but frozen isn't too great a problem. Most commercial pudding is made with dried blood, which is easily found. This needs to be reconstituted. The instructions will say with water, but in my experience milk gives a better result.

400g best-quality pork back fat – *I use the fat from loins of rare-breed pigs, which always seem to have too much*

450g onions – *finely chopped*

4 small apples, *peeled, cored and diced*

50g fresh breadcrumbs

500ml pork blood

100ml double cream

4 teaspoons coarse sea salt

1 teaspoon freshly ground black pepper

1 teaspoon ground cinnamon

2 tablespoons brandy

1 tablespoon Worcestershire sauce

Preheat the oven to 160°C/fan 140°C/gas mark 3.

Place the pork fat in a pan over a low heat until some starts to render.

Add the onions and apples. When cooked, add the breadcrumbs and leave to cool.

Blend in a food processer with the blood, cream and seasonings. Pour this mixture into a 23cm square deep-sided roasting tin, then place the tin in a larger roasting tray half filled with warm water.

Bake for about 1 hour until firm, then leave to cool.

# Calf's kidney with parsley and mustard sauce

FOR 4

Lamb's kidneys are nice, but calf's are nicer. If the kidneys are dark, then they will need to be soaked in a 50/50 mixture of milk and water for 1 hour, then patted dry. (Too much blood makes too strong a dish for this hour of the day and the soaking will remove a reasonable amount.)

Any sort of kidney will have a tight set of white membrane at its centre. This will mutate into dental floss if left in as it takes longer to cook than the surrounding kidney meat. If using lamb's kidney, then the solution is simple. Cut the kidney in half, then cut away the white membrane. Calf's kidney takes a little longer and more effort but is largely the same process. Once the membrane has been cut away, sear the kidney on each side in a hot oiled saucepan, leave to settle for a few minutes, then cut into large dice. When needed, these dice can be quickly and evenly cooked so that there is no blue or raw part but still a pink interior to the meat.

. . . . . . . . . . . . . . . . . . . . . . . . . . . . . . . . . . . . . . . . . . . . . . . . . . . . . . . . . . . . . . . . .

1 calf's kidney or 8 lamb's kidneys, split and trimmed of internal membrane

Vegetable oil

1 tablespoon wholegrain mustard

4 tablespoons crème fraîche

2 tablespoons chopped flat-leaf parsley

Salt and freshly ground black pepper

Heat a pan until you think it has become too hot.

Brush the kidney with oil, then season with salt and black pepper. Fry the kidney for a few moments, then add the mustard.

When the mustard is cooked – just a few moments – add the crème fraîche and parsley.

Serve on toast or with griddled Irish potato bread.

# VEGETABLE DISHES & VEGETARIAN DISHES

## ARE NOT ALWAYS IDENTICAL

There are two distinct aspects to vegetable cookery: dishes in which a vegetable is centre stage, and side dishes, which are there to complement some piece of protein – the two veg in the 'meat and two veg' arrangement. In fact, one of the two veg will always be starch, perhaps potato, rice or noodles. The starch is essential to the balance of the meal, giving the comfort element and providing bulk. The other vegetables are peripheral at best and often superfluous. Side vegetables should only be there if they contribute something to the dish. Carrots and peas, or carrots and broccoli, are regularly served alongside some piece of fish or meat purely to fulfil a pedestrian colour scheme rather than a gap in the taste or nutritional spectrum.

## Side vegetables should only be there if they contribute something to the dish.

Dishes that are meat- and fish-free usually revolve around the starch, maybe as a pasta, pilaf or pastry confection. In fact, this solves a problem because some green vegetables have lots of texture and flavour but little presence or impact. Some young broad beans and girolle mushrooms will make a superb tagliatelle, peas and rice go together perfectly, and spiced roast root vegetables make a heart-warming tart on a winter's day.

Most fruit and vegetables are seasonal. That said, the boundaries of each variety's season will be constantly expanding through improved horticultural techniques and selective breeding of strains that are resistant to disease and earlier or later cropping. Air freighting should mean that fruit and veg harvested in the southern hemisphere can reach the shops here as quickly as it would have from the home country. All this isn't the Enid Blyton or Walt Disney style of happy outcome it should be. Many of the varieties grown are for the benefit of the transport business rather than the consumer, and anyone who has eaten exotic fruits in Latin America will realise that the fine-looking specimens of dragon fruit and tomatillo that we can buy here are tasteless by comparison. Our own apples and pears are bred and harvested for uniformity rather than flavour. All this is our own fault. There is no point blaming the supermarkets – they merely supply what we demand. Even so, the range of produce on offer year round would have astounded the shoppers of the 1950s and '60s. My childhood in central London offered only a tiny choice of tired and badly stored vegetables and a trip to Soho was needed if exotica such as green or red peppers were called for. There were butchers and greengrocers on every high street, but not necessarily great ones.

Yesterday's solutions to the seasonal gluts of fruit and vegetables gave us jams and pickles, dried pulses and sauerkraut. The canning and bottling industries gave us more choice, but are best considered as store cupboard items, then of course came Clarence Birdseye and the frozen food business. Each had successes which outlived the original needs. The jury is still out on irradiated fruit, not because it is inherently dangerous, but more because it allows even more careless treatment of whatever is being treated, usually raspberries.

# SIDE VEGETABLES

These should contribute something to the meal rather than take up space on the plate. They should be considered in conjunction with whatever else they will be sharing space with. The inevitable duo of broccoli and carrot doesn't do anything for most dishes. Similarly, think about the amount of starch that you are serving now that plated meals rather than side bowls are the norm. Well-brought-up people will want to finish whatever is on the plate, so if you have too much or too little mashed potato, the pleasure will be diminished. The same goes for any sauce you are serving.

Years back, the problem with green vegetables was overcooking. More recently it has been the reverse, with brightly coloured but hard French beans and carrots challenging your expensive dentistry and adding little to your enjoyment. The guide is that green vegetables like the bean and cabbage family should be cooked in lots of boiling salted water so that the water will reboil faster. Overloading the pan doesn't help with either speed or retaining vibrant colour or texture. Spinach, of course, is the exception as it produces so much liquid itself. Just put it into a pan with a few drops of water or butter and cover with a lid so that the steam from its own juices do the cooking.

The more you cook something, the more its flavour comes through, whether it's braised beef or roasted carrots. If you want the crunch of celeriac or carrot, then serve it thinly sliced and raw. If you want a deep, sweet taste, then cook it through. If it doesn't look so gorgeous, then purée it, which gives an opportunity for adding butter or cream or cooking liquor from whatever else is being made.

An interesting vegetable transforms a dish so that no fancy footwork is needed with sauces or marinades. Cauliflower florets fried with lots of Middle Eastern spices like cumin, coriander and cinnamon, then finished with a little stock or white wine and a handful of chopped parsley and coriander will turn a plainly grilled piece of lamb or chicken into an event. A creamy gratin dauphinoise or spiced carrot purée will do likewise. And so will petits pois à la française, a combination of tinned petits pois, drained almost but not completely, then heated and finished with crisp lardons of streaky bacon, strips of lettuce, fried small or chopped onion and the stirring in of a good piece of unsalted butter, as much as you might think appropriate then doubled, to make a sauce as well as a vegetable. This is the traditional partner to roast pigeon and duck, but will be great with chicken or lamb, or even by itself with warm crusty bread. Fresh or frozen peas will not substitute; tinned are the real deal. Savoy cabbage is the king of brassica, great texture and a deep flavour that no other variety has ever matched. If you want to make more of it, try cutting it into strips and cooking it in a mixture of a little goose fat and a little water – diced smoked bacon an optional extra.

> An interesting vegetable transforms a dish so that no fancy footwork is needed with sauces or marinades.

# Fried artichokes with tomato and olive salad

Deep-fried artichoke is a Sephardic Jewish dish popular in Italy. The artichokes need precooking in water and olive oil in order to be soft enough for final deep-frying. Small or baby artichokes are called for and all this other tomato and olive stuff is just optional to make the artichokes look more of an event.

FOR 4

8 small artichokes

Juice of 2 lemons

50ml cheap olive oil

Oil *for frying*

4 slices of sourdough bread

20 pitted green olives

4 large pitted black olives

2 tablespoons *grated* Pecorino

1 tablespoon good-quality olive oil

1 tablespoon *coarsely chopped* flat-leaf parsley

4 large ripe tomatoes

Freshly ground black pepper

Cut away the stalks of the artichokes, then pare off the coarser outer leaves. A baby artichoke will be very soft and need little trimming. Brush each with the lemon juice, then cover with the cheap olive oil and water in a small pan. Poach for 15–20 minutes until they are soft. Drain and leave to cool, then use a small spoon to scoop out the hairy choke from the middle of each one. Deep-fry in hot oil at 180°C until golden brown.

Grill the bread. Chop the olives, then mix with the Pecorino, good olive oil and parsley. Season with a few drops of the lemon juice and black pepper.

Slice the tomatoes and arrange across the toast. Spoon over the olive mix, then serve with two deep-fried artichokes per person.

# Twice-baked Lancashire cheese soufflés

FOR 6

Twice-baked soufflés are easy and very good to eat. The general idea is that you cook the soufflés, which by the way will not rise much, then turn them out of their dish. Ten minutes before they are needed, place the unmoulded soufflés on a baking tray and bake in a hot oven until crisp on the outside. Most hard cheeses like Cheddar work fine, as does goat's cheese. The best is Lancashire. Served with a spoonful of beetroot salad and a few dressed green leaves, it will make an ideal first course. I use Shurrock's Lancashire Bomber, which is a soft, fruity cheese. Use ramekin dishes or dariole moulds, the metal containers in which crème caramels are made. The major pitfall will be the moulds. If they are not slathered with butter the soufflés will not rise. I smear generous amounts of butter inside each mould, then refrigerate them and repeat the process afterwards. Never fails.

There are of course lots of variations on this recipe anyway. Goat's cheese, a mixture of mashed swede and Cheddar, or the addition of morel mushrooms or deep-fried sage leaves all work well. As with any soufflé, whether twice-baked or the standard type, the key will be strong and dominating flavours. Anything muted will stand no chance against all that whisked egg white.

350ml whole milk

50g unsalted butter

50g plain flour

6g cornflour

4 egg yolks

1 teaspoon English mustard

1 teaspoon Worcestershire sauce

6 egg whites – *whisked until stiff*

250g *crumbled* Lancashire cheese

Dash of Tabasco sauce

Salt and freshly ground black pepper

Preheat the oven to 180°C/fan 160°C/gas mark 4.

Heat the milk in a small saucepan.

Make beurre manié with the butter and flour – that is, soften the butter and work the flour into it to form a thick, smooth paste.

Whisk the beurre manié into the warm milk, then bring to the boil.

Turn off the heat, then stir in the cornflour and egg yolks, then the mustard and Worcestershire sauce.

Fold in the egg white, then add the cheese and seasonings.

Butter the ramekins, then spoon in the mixture. Place the ramekins in a deep roasting tray half-filled with water, then bake for about 15 minutes until risen. Remove from the oven and turn out onto a lined baking tray.

When needed, bake the soufflés again for about 15 minutes until hot and crisp.

Serve with boiled asparagus in May, well-dressed salads any time or diced baked beetroot with horseradish flakes in winter.

# Asparagus with quail egg and mushroom scotch eggs

FOR 4

Asparagus used to be sold by the 'round of "gras"', 'gras' meaning fat, and they would have more or less spears, depending on their thickness. When I lived in Evesham, which still is a big asparagus-growing area, the pubs and restaurants all offered steamed or poached 'gras' with melted butter during the season. Hollandaise sauce is the usual partner, but fresh goat's cheese and a decent salad dressing will work well too. It's important in this dish that the egg isn't too cooked as the runny yolk will act as a sauce.

There are two main styles of asparagus: white and green. The white variety will have been earthed up as it grows to protect the vegetable from sunlight. Mounding up the soil in this way blanches the stem white. Young crowns of asparagus produce feathery stems called sprue, which are usually cheaper. The base of older asparagus stems will have fungal spores, so cut them off. The bases are regularly woody in any case and the way you can tell how far down to shorten the spears is to bend each stem until it snaps. This is a touch untidy so a good guess is to lose the bottom third. Peeling or not peeling is a matter of personal preference. Mine is to peel the stems two-thirds of the way up. This ensures more even cooking so you can tuck into almost all the vegetable.

6 quail's eggs

2 shallots

300g mushrooms

1 tablespoon *chopped* flat-leaf parsley

100g fresh breadcrumbs – panko is fine

1 egg – *beaten*

20 asparagus spears – *trimmed and peeled*

Salt and freshly ground black pepper

Bring a saucepan of water to the boil. Gently lower in the quail's eggs and, when the water returns to the boil, time them for 2½ minutes. Lift the quail's eggs into a container of cold water and leave to cool. They will be quite soft so a great deal of care is needed when you shell them – maybe cook an extra couple of eggs just in case.

Finely chop the shallots and mushrooms. Cook until dry – the mushrooms will lose liquid and bubble. Season to taste, add the parsley and 1 tablespoonful of the fresh breadcrumbs – the stuffing has to be firm enough to coat the eggs – and leave to cool. For each quail's egg place 1 tablespoon of stuffing onto clingfilm, pat out until flat, then place an egg in the centre. Use the clingfilm to wrap the stuffing around the egg, then refrigerate until firm. Eggwash and breadcrumb the scotch eggs. When needed, deep-fry at 180°C until brown and crisp, then place in a hot oven to heat right through for a few minutes.

VEGETABLE DISHES & VEGETARIAN DISHES ARE NOT ALWAYS IDENTICAL

Meanwhile, bring a large saucepan of salted water to the boil and cook the asparagus until tender – time varies according to the thickness of the stems, but 3 or 4 minutes should be enough.

Lay the asparagus onto warmed plates. Cut the scotch eggs in half and place three halves on top of each portion.

## HERBS AND SPICES

Both are flavourings but there is a difference. Fresh herbs need only a short contact with heat at most and, whatever the underlying taste, will lend a fresh, clean and lively finish to a dish. Never use fresh herbs at the start of a slow-cooked dish or let them cook out in something hot for more than a few moments. The fragile scents will be lost completely. Don't waste parsley by scattering it over whatever you feel looks dull in the savoury line. And don't chop, or tear if you're using basil, too finely or too far in advance.

Dried herbs are best thought of as spices and used accordingly. They need cooking to restore their flavour and in fact the flavour imparted is significantly different from the fresh. Dried oregano, Greek rigani, is more useful than fresh and combines with cinnamon and allspice to produce the moussaka you want, similarly combines with garlic, cumin and paprika for perfect gulyas. Dried parsley and thyme aren't so clever and taste like those post-war packet stuffing mixes we all want to forget.

Spices are complex – some are hot, others fragrant. Warm flavours like cinnamon and even cumin are best added late to a dish while most others cook into a dish subtly affecting the final taste. Most spices are best dry-roasted then pulverised in a grinder. This takes enthusiasm, which you may find lacking but will give a sharper edge to your dish. Ground spices are fine of course, provided you bin the packet's leftovers after a few weeks rather than months or years.

# Chickpea and olive oil soup

FOR 6

Pulses, the pea and bean family, give depth, body and satisfaction to meatless dishes. They soak up butter and goose fat, but also partner olive oil perfectly. Pythagoras (he of the pi r squared) founded a religious cult that believed in the transmigration of the soul after death. He was a vegetarian and his followers evoked great derision when they offered up bunches of salad and vegetable at the altars of the gods. He also believed that the devils that live below ground could make their way up the hollow stems of the pulse family. So they couldn't eat them either. Small wonder the cult didn't last as long as the theorem. But no excuse for my own failed Maths O level.

This dish isn't vegetarian, but could be with a little harmless tweaking. Bean soups – potage Saint-Germain, fresh pea soup, the minestrones and menestras – are all fabulously satisfying in a way that most soups are not. They also don't need a bunch of salts and chemicals to help things along. Make consommé and you will need skill, perfect stock and patience. Make bean soup and you will need just an appetite and maybe some crusty bread.

Pulses used only to come dried. It's still cheaper that way but you have no idea how long they have been stored and so how long they will need soaking and cooking. In general, large chickpeas are better than small, but a tin will do the job perfectly here.

240g tin chickpeas

1 chicken leg – *skin on*

1 large onion – *chopped*

2 large garlic cloves – *chopped*

1 large leek – *chopped*

1 teaspoon each ground cinnamon, cumin and coriander

6 tablespoons olive oil

100ml white wine

1 tablespoon lemon juice

1 tablespoon *chopped* coriander leaves

Salt and freshly ground black pepper

Drain the chickpeas – evidently the well-known side effects of the bean family are mitigated this way. Place in a large pot with the chicken leg, vegetables and spices. Add 1 litre of cold water, then bring to the boil. Simmer for about 25 minutes until the chicken is cooked.

Lift out the chicken leg, then scrape all the meat off the bone. Return the meat to the pot and liquidise the lot in a blender, adding half the olive oil, the wine, seasoning and lemon. If the soup needs thickening, add more oil; if it's too thick, add a little water or more wine.

Serve the soup with ½ tablespoon of olive oil and some chopped coriander leaves.

Now of course you can also add boiled vegetables, maybe sliced runner beans or cauliflower florets. I have also used langoustines and lobsters in the past.

# Celeriac puddings with wild mushrooms

Celeriac and wild mushrooms work well together, and the same method and proportions can be used with carrots or parsnips. I have served this as a stand-alone dish and also alongside venison or hare to make a grander dish for the restaurant. Try to use common sense when making this dish. You cannot usually buy a specific weight of celeriac, only some vague approximation, so add or subtract a little cream if necessary. If you cannot get wild mushrooms, then use slices of open flat mushroom and maybe some dried morels or porcini, soaked and sliced.

FOR 4 AS A STARTER
OR 6 AS A SIDE

. . . . . . . . . . . . . . . . . . . . . . . . . . . . . . . . . . . . . . . . . . . . . . . . . . . . . . . . . . . . . . . . . . . . . . . . . . . . . . . . . . . . . . . .

1 medium celeriac – *peeled*

150ml double cream

2 eggs

1 teaspoon creamed horseradish

350g wild mushrooms

50ml olive oil, plus extra for brushing

100ml white wine

Salt and freshly ground black pepper

Preheat the oven to 160°C/fan 140°/gas mark 3.

Dice and boil the celeriac until soft. Don't worry if it discolours slightly. Drain, then leave to cool.

Blend in a food processor adding the cream, eggs, horseradish and seasoning.

Line ramekin dishes or individual moulds with food-friendly clingfilm and brush with oil. Pipe or spoon in the celeriac mixture, then tap each dish so that the vegetable reaches all the bottom edges.

Place in a roasting tray half filled with warm water for about 20 minutes, then bake until set. Check by pressing lightly on a pudding with your fingertips.

To make the sauce, gently fry the mushrooms in the oil. Scoop onto kitchen paper, then add the white wine and seasoning to the pan and any leftover olive oil to warm before blending. Blend in a liquidiser.

Turn out the puddings onto warmed plates. Dab away any excess juices, then scatter the mushrooms around and dress with the warm sauce.

# Garlic and lemon courgettes with girolle mushrooms and crème fraîche

FOR 4

Courgettes are available all year round but they aren't good all year round. Recently harvested, they are delicately flavoured and crunchy. Chilled and stored for air freighting across the globe, they turn dry and coarse. During the summer, they are worthy of extra effort and will make an interesting starter. Their usual accompaniment is tomato, but later in the season when the first wild mushrooms appear they can be given this treatment.

My introduction to mushroom-gathering came during my first job as Head Chef at the Montcalm, from my Italian sous chef, Luigi, who showed me a series of places in parks around London where they were to be found. Those who gather wild mushrooms have one thing in common – secrecy – because such foraged delights tend to reappear in the same spots each season, and to tell another is to find an empty space where once there may have been a kilo of girolles, hedgehog mushrooms or cèpes. It's 25 years since Luigi and I worked together and he is long since retired, but I receive a card each Christmas from him still with a detailed report on the mushroom season and even, occasionally, a few new places to find them.

8 small courgettes

Olive oil, for brushing

1 tablespoon *chopped* parsley

1 tablespoon *finely shredded* basil

1 small garlic clove – *crushed*

A little grated lemon zest

50g unsalted butter – *softened*

100g girolle mushrooms

10g unsalted butter

1 shallot – *finely chopped*

25ml white wine

50ml crème fraîche

Salt and freshly ground black pepper

Split each courgette lengthways, then brush with olive oil, season with salt and black pepper, and grill or griddle. This will take only 3–4 minutes each side.

Work the parsley, basil, garlic and lemon zest into the soft butter so that they are well mixed. Brush the cooked courgettes with about half the herb butter.

Halve each girolle and cook in the butter along with the shallot. Season with salt and black pepper, then add the wine and crème fraîche. Bring to the boil. Whisk in the remaining herb butter.

Serve the grilled courgettes on a small pool of girolle sauce.

The butter in the recipe is used in two stages, first to flavour the grilled courgette, then to thicken the sauce. It should be soft but not melted.

This recipe would particularly suit a barbecue because the searing would be ideal as a cooking method and the black markings from a charcoal grill look attractive on the vegetables. The sauce may not, of course, be sufficiently coarse for something as macho as a barbecue. You could always pretend that there are a lot of chillies involved...

VEGETABLE DISHES & VEGETARIAN DISHES ARE NOT ALWAYS IDENTICAL

# MUSHROOMS

There is little tradition in Britain of gathering wild mushrooms – most people you spot searching will be Italian or Polish – so the names by which wild mushrooms are known have only recently begun to settle. The Boletus mushrooms, previously called Penny Buns, became cèpes and then porcini, as first French and then Italian recipes referred to them in their own language. Girolles used to be known as chanterelles – their Latin name – but now this name has been affixed to a different mushroom, much inferior and entirely unrelated.

There is an old wives' tale that you should never wash mushrooms. Those who like gritty food will be okay, but for the rest of us it is good to give them a quick dunk in cold water. Provided they are dried swiftly afterwards there will be no harm done. Any mushroom left wet will of course become soggy quite quickly.

# POTATOES

Potatoes have their origin in South America. A visit to the island of Chiloé off the coast of southern Chile, the place where they are meant to originate from, shows why they might have been such a success in places like Ireland. I visited in midsummer when the rain poured down on to a dull cool day. Potatoes grew wild in hundreds of varieties, and the favourite local dish involved steaming these spuds and fish over a broth, the three components combining to make a hearty lunch.

It is possible to differentiate potatoes by colour – mostly red or white – but more useful to think in terms of density, from waxy to floury. Floury, soft-textured potatoes are the best for roasting and chips. King Edward is the variety that has stayed popular and available the longest. Then there is a progression of varieties that are all-purpose, making serviceable chips and usable mash. In Ireland, floury spuds are used for mash as well. I prefer the result these give. In France, there was a much-copied trend to use waxy potatoes like Ratte for mash, the idea being that firm potatoes will withstand much more butter and cream. They do but it's not necessarily an improvement.

New potatoes, especially the magnificent Jersey Royals, produce the finest in the waxy, dense style, certainly better than the year-round midget varieties like Charlotte. These are always best when boiled and served whole, but are useful sliced in gratins and suchlike when their ability to retain texture when cooked is handy.

# Potatoes and taleggio

FOR 4

I cut out this tallegio recipe from a newspaper years ago and think that it came from Rowley Leigh. The recipe on the following page, Janssen's temptation, is popular all over Scandinavia and calls for my favourite store cupboard item, anchovies. Neither dishes are vegetarian but both make interesting use of potatoes.

. . . . . . . . . . . . . . . . . . . . . . . . . . . . . . . . . . . . . . . . . . . . . . . . . . . . . . . . . . . . . . . . . . . . . . . .

5 medium potatoes – *not too floury as they will disintegrate*

Olive oil

225g taleggio – *sliced into rounds the thickness of a pound coin*

5 thin rashers of streaky bacon or pancetta, *cut into short strips*

70g Parmesan – *grated*

Salt and freshly ground black pepper

Preheat the oven to 180°C/fan 160°C/gas mark 4.

Boil the potatoes in their skins. When they are cooked through, drain then leave to cool.

Peel then cut into thinnish rounds.

Drizzle some olive oil into a deep ovenproof dish. Season the potatoes and Taleggio with salt and black pepper. Lay this into the dish, along with the bacon. Scatter Parmesan on top and a few drops more olive oil.

Bake for 20 minutes, or until the potatoes have started to crisp.

# Jansson's temptation

FOR 8

This is my favourite potato dish. Jansson is the Swedish equivalent of Jones so the name may well just mean everyone's temptation. The idea is similar to the French gratin dauphinoise, but with anchovy rather than grated cheese. The result is more savoury than fishy. I use mussel juice when I have it, but any stock, will add to the dish and if you have no stock then water and a little of the pickling liquor will be fine, as would plain milk.

The anchovies called for are the silvery jobs rather than the brown ones, but either or both together will produce a creditable result. Spanish boquerones would be perfect, if these are easier to find. All give a fine, if slightly different, result.

The finished dish should be a touch crisp. If it helps, then either a sprinkling of fresh breadcrumbs or a few dots of butter across the top will achieve that effect.

Watch out for the seasoning. Anchovies are salty, so put in less than you would for a gratin dauphinoise.

1.2kg maincrop potatoes – *peeled and cut into batons*

1 onion – *finely chopped*

12 anchovy fillets

400ml hot stock or whole milk

1 litre double cream

Preheat the oven to 180°C/fan 160°C/gas mark 4

Season the potatoes, then turn in a bowl with the onion and anchovies. Spoon into an ovenproof dish and pour over the stock/milk and the cream.

Cover with foil and bake for about 1½ hours until soft.

Remove the foil, return to the oven and continue to bake until starting to crisp.

Allow to rest for 10 minutes before serving.

VEGETABLE DISHES & VEGETARIAN DISHES ARE NOT ALWAYS IDENTICAL

# Salad cream

FOR 6

Salad cream always meant either Heinz or Crosse & Blackwell's oversweet commercial product. Properly made, however, it is a revelation. Serve with a salad made from Webbs or Cos lettuce, tomatoes, radishes, cucumber, watercress, hard-boiled eggs and spring onions.

2 hard-boiled eggs

1 tablespoon Dijon mustard

1 tablespoon caster sugar

Salt freshly ground black pepper and a pinch of cayenne or a dash of Tabasco sauce

1 tablespoon lemon juice

150ml double cream

Mash the egg yolks with 1 teaspoon of cold water, then incorporate the mustard, sugar, seasonings and lemon juice.

Trickle the cream into this paste while stirring continuously. Taste and add more lemon, salt or sugar as needed. I'm too mean to throw away the egg whites from the salad cream ingredients, so slice them and mix them into the salad ingredients mentioned in the introduction before spooning over the salad cream.

Webbs Wonderful is an exceptional variety of lettuce first developed by Webbs of Wychbold in the West Midlands. It is now only available if you grow it yourself, but is well worth it, being similar to iceberg lettuce but with flavour as well as crunch.

## SALADS

What's a salad, I hear you ask? Are lettuces obligatory or does the term mean something else? The word used to imply a cold dish dressed with something piquant and refreshing, but there are warm salads with hot bits amongst the cold. And don't even think about fruit salad. My childhood memories are of dreaded dull confections, mostly round lettuce with chunks of tomato, cucumber and boiled egg. Essentially, there is nothing wrong with this apart from the absence of a proper dressing to make it edible. Salad without dressing is rabbit food. The dressing makes the salad.

# Puntarelle salad with anchovy and garlic dressing

FOR 4

The choice of salad leaves has improved dramatically. Bitter winter leaves from the endive family are available most of the year and will give some crunch to the dish. Frisée lettuce from this family is the only bore, tasting like hedge trimmings, but appears often as it is attractive to look at and comparatively cheap. For reasons I don't understand, puntarelle is still only available from November to March. The plant is a form of chicory and comprises leaves and shoots. The shoots, small cartridge-like growths, are the business. They need to be cut off and then soaked in cold water for about 24 hours until they curl.

The dressing is what makes the salad, of course. We make anchovy sticks, like cheese straws only with anchovy as well, but warm croutons will be fine. A head of puntarelle is quite large, so cut it in half if it is too much.

### Dressing

1 tin anchovy fillets (brown ones)

50ml olive oil

20g *crushed* garlic

Freshly ground black pepper

1 tablespoon red wine vinegar

### Salad

1 puntarelle

1 small, moderately hot chilli – *thinly sliced*

Parmesan shavings

4 anchovy fillets – from the tin used for the dressing

Croutons, cheese straws or anchovy sticks

For the dressing, finely chop 25g of the anchovy fillets. Slice 4 fillets in half lengthways and reserve for the salad.

Heat the oil, then add the garlic and cook to golden brown.

Remove from the heat, then add the chopped anchovies, black pepper and vinegar. Leave the dressing to cool.

Drain and dry the puntarelle shoots. Tip into a bowl, add the chilli and spoon on some dressing. Toss together, then spoon into salad dishes. Scatter Parmesan shavings, the sliced anchovies and croutons on top.

VEGETABLE DISHES & VEGETARIAN DISHES ARE NOT ALWAYS IDENTICAL

# 4

## SEA FISH IS WAY

# SUPERIOR

## TO FRESHWATER

Fish is controversial. Not just for the problems of sustainability, overfishing and pollution. Britain is an island surrounded by great fishing grounds, but really we don't like or eat the stuff if there is meat to be had instead. It's not a point of view the rest of the world shares, and the rest of the world in this case will have the pleasure of fish in all its variety. The range is vast, from white-fleshed species like sole and turbot to oily herrings and mackerel. Then there is seafood such as squid and octopus, prawns and lobster, scallops and mussels, and smoked and salted fish, kippers and haddock, eels and salmon, plus fish roe like bottarga and caviar. Surely even the most timid eater will find something amongst all these? Interestingly, the Baltic countries love fish too, though they have to make do with freshwater fish and the small range of sea fish that breed in the low saline waters of the Baltic. Chefs, on the other hand, love cooking fish, especially white flat fish, because they are wonderful vehicles for the cook's craftsmanship.

Sea fish is way superior to freshwater. The great river fish are salmon and sea trout, which both spend large parts of their life cycle at sea. Middle and Eastern European countries far from a seashore will enjoy carp and zander, even pike. But these are all bony creatures with subdued flavour and none can compare with a large sea bass or turbot for texture or taste.

> Fish is controversial. Not just for the problems of sustainability, overfishing and pollution.

## BUYING AND STORING FISH

Availability and price vary dramatically from day to day. Stormy weather will keep the fishermen at home and the fluctuations of supply and demand, maybe a banquet in London's Park Lane that calls for 500g soles for 1,000 people, can warp the market. Always best to shop within a style of fish, so buy brill if there's no turbot, haddock if there's no cod. There is no longer such a thing as cheap fish, so all will have some cachet at the dining table. Fishmongers have all but disappeared and supermarkets where I live have yet to overcome the difficulties of stocking products that deteriorate quickly, and whose prices fluctuate daily. They are always going to be happier negotiating long-term price deals for stuff that comes with a good shelf life and prefer to deal just in fish like farmed salmon and prawns that have almost limitless availability. Your eyes must be your guide to freshness: shiny skin rather than flat, dry flesh. If it's any consolation, buying at the quayside fish markets is no guarantee either. Trawlers will be out fishing for a week or more and catching most days, so the skill of the trawlermen in icing down each netful of fish will be crucial if the catch is to look fresh when the boat gets back to port.

The last water a fish should see after it leaves the ocean, river or lake should be the poaching liquor you use to cook it. Water, even liquid that seeps from the fish itself, will dry out the flesh and age the fish faster. Pat the fish dry before refrigerating it and cover with clingfilm to keep out the air. If you intend keeping it for longer than a day, repeat the process periodically. Mussels and lobster are the exception, of course, as they should still be alive and will need to be kept damp and cool.

The great Mediterranean civilisation of ancient Greece covered most of the eastern seaboard, including the coast of Egypt and the lands that fringe the Black Sea as well as the islands of Cyprus and Sicily. Meat was eaten, of course, but not regularly, and would have been slaughtered, cooked and distributed according to rank and seniority by a specialised semi-religious group known as mageiros (the same word meant priest, butcher and cook). Most of the time it was fish that was the centrepiece of an important meal. There were strict rules over freshness and contemporary accounts of rogue fish sellers pretending to faint so that they – and the fish – could be revived with buckets of water. The classical version of Elizabeth David was a Sicilian Greek called Archestratus who wrote about fish in the fourth century BC. He advised the prime time of year for tuna and which cuts were best. Fatty was much prized and the belly was the most sought after. He also advised against allowing Italians near your sea bass as they had a tendency to cover the fish with cheese and pickle. There is still a translation and commentary of his work in print. Well, in fact it is written by myself and Professor John Wilkins from Exeter University. Cannot wait to read it, I hear you say.

## FISH COOKERY

Fish is delicate, so clumsy handling isn't appropriate. The general rule for fish cookery is a light touch. In most treatments, a balance between fat or oil and acid – lemon, wine or vinegar – is the key. Forget notions that lemon partners fish automatically. Lemon cuts through the fattiness of the deep-frying process or pan-fried fish that has seen a lot of butter or olive oil but generally it is the sauce partnering the fish that needs the balancing with something acidic rather than the fish itself.

Steamed fish is missing oil or butter, so sauces derived from hollandaise (see page 31) or beurre blanc work best. Poached fish produces its own stock, which it would be daft to waste. A little butter and flour mixed together and whisked into the stock will produce a creditable base for whatever herbs, cream or wine you want to add.

Fried fish has had all the oil it needs during cooking, so some sort of relish, maybe a tomato sauce, will be wanted. Butter sauce on top of fried fish will taste greasy.

Raw fish (sashimi, ceviche, tartares and the like) aren't really raw at all; they are as cooked by lime juice, soy and the rest, as anything fried. If you brush a thin slice of raw salmon with lemon or lime juice and season it, the result will be very palatable alongside some salad or dip. Leave it another 5 minutes and you'll notice the fish has changed texture, looking cooked.

> The last water a fish should see after it leaves the ocean, river or lake should be the poaching liquor you use to cook it.

All this kid-glove handling and light touch stuff is called for with delicate-fleshed fish, but there are moments when big flavours and spicing will hit the spot.

# Tandoori fish

FOR 6

Most of us in Britain would credit the post-war boom in Indian restaurants for our early restaurant experiences. And there are now brilliant chefs from the Indian subcontinent, the likes of Atul Kochar, Cyrus Todiwala and Vineet Bhatia, showing what glorious regional tastes the area can deliver. Sadly, though, most restaurants are pretty grim and have settled for providing mediocre post-drinking fodder for the cheapest possible price. Time maybe to remember what a vibrant cuisine we are dealing with and then perhaps to move on from the customary hotchpotch of dishes from northern India and Pakistan to look at the food of southern India and Sri Lanka as well. This recipe is an interesting take on the usual tandoori treatment. It works best with solid-textured, comparatively good-value fish such as stone bass or pollack. Kashmiri chilli powder is sold in most supermarkets. It's a lot milder than standard chilli powder, so don't substitute the latter unless you fancy a nuclear experience at dinner time

6 x 200g stone bass fillets

25g butter

1 tablespoon *chopped* coriander leaves

1 tablespoon lime juice

**Raita**

100g plain full-fat yogurt

½ teaspoon salt

1 teaspoon lime juice

Salad, *to garnish*

**PASTE**

*Dry spices*

3 teaspoons cumin seeds

3 teaspoons black peppercorns

6 cardamom pods – just the seeds

2 teaspoons cloves

*Wet spices*

2 small chillies

4 large garlic cloves

1 small knob of ginger – *peeled and chopped*

3 teaspoons salt

2 tablespoons Kashmiri chilli powder

6 tablespoons plain full-fat yogurt

6 tablespoons vegetable oil

Heat the dry spices in a dry pan, then blend in a spice grinder. Blend the wet spices with 25ml of water in a liquidiser, then add the dry spices and mix to a paste. Turn the fish in the paste and marinate for at least 2 hours.

When you are ready to cook, preheat the grill and mix together the ingredients for the raita in a small bowl. Lay the fillets on a roasting tin and dot with the butter. Grill until done. The timing will depend on the thickness of your fish fillets, but 10 minutes is a good guide.

Sprinkle with the coriander and lime juice. Serve with salad leaves and the raita.

# Kerala fish curry

FOR 6

Kerala is the great fishing area of southern India. There are sea-fishing fleets, of course, but more interestingly there are miles of backwaters with brackish water as well as freshwater lakes, all of which support different kinds of fish. These are all harvested and the most prized is the Pearl Spot fish from the brackish waters. Keralans use tamarind as a souring agent rather than lime juice in their cooking, but it is in most other respects similar to Southeast Asian cuisines like Thai or Vietnamese. This recipe covers all options by using both.

There's not a lot of Pearl Spot in South Wales where I work so whichever fish you fancy will substitute just fine. My preference is for a meaty fish like gurnard or sea bream as it will take the spicing really well. Waste of money to use sole or turbot.

Like most Asian dishes, this recipe calls for a vast range of spices and herbs. Don't be daunted – the same spices constitute the paste and most of the sauce. A word about chillies: a general rule is that the smaller the angrier. So, scotch bonnets and bird's eye chillies will be dynamite, whereas padrón or jalapeño chillies will be almost pleasant enough to chew. If in any doubt, use Tabasco.

· · · · · · · · · · · · · · · · · · · · · · · · · · · · · · · · · · · · · · · · · · · · · · · · · · · · · · · · · · · · · · · · · · · · · · · · · · · · · · · ·

6 x 150g gurnard fillets

25g butter

Salt

**Paste**

1 medium onion – *chopped*

6 garlic cloves – *chopped*

1 small knob of ginger – *peeled and chopped*

1 small green chilli – *chopped*

1 tablespoon ground cumin

1 tablespoon ground coriander

½ teaspoon ground turmeric

½ teaspoon ground fenugreek

Two hours in advance, blend all the paste ingredients in a food-processor or liquidiser. Spread two-thirds of the result over the fish fillets and marinate until needed, but for at least 30 minutes.

For the curry, heat the oil in a large pan and fry the onion, chilli, tomatoes, mustard seeds, curry leaves and the remaining paste until brown, then add the stock or water, tamarind paste and coconut milk. Simmer for a few moments, then leave off the heat until needed. Anything with coconut milk will tend to split if cooked too long at a high temperature.

Thirty minutes in advance, warm the curry sauce.

Heat a frying pan with the butter, then season the fish with salt and sear quickly on each side. Work in batches, one or two at a time, so that the coating cooks and colours.

½ teaspoon freshly ground black pepper – *the long black pepper of the region is good if you can source it*

1 tablespoon tomato passata

2 tablespoons coconut or vegetable oil

Pinch of salt

### Curry

1 tablespoon vegetable oil

1 small onion – *chopped*

1 small chilli – *chopped*

2 medium tomatoes – *roughly chopped*

1 teaspoon mustard seeds

6 curry leaves

250ml stock or water

1 tablespoon tamarind paste

400ml tin coconut milk

1 tablespoon lime juice

2 tablespoons *chopped* flat-leaf parsley

2 tablespoons *chopped* coriander

Lift the fish into the simmering sauce. The timing will now depend on the thickness of the fish fillets, but a guide of 15 minutes should work. Stir in the lime juice, parsley and coriander.

Serve in bowls or deep plates as the sauce will not be particularly thick.

# Mouclade

FOR 6

This curried mussels dish can be used as a backdrop to some prime specimen like turbot or bass. Just grill the fish and lay it on top of the mouclade. It's rather fine just as it is though and an interesting change from moules marinières where the mussels are cooked in much the same way but without the spicing. Mussels have a full and distinctive flavour that can stand up to most treatments and win. At Carriers restaurant in the seventies we used them often, sometimes poached then coated with soft garlic butter back in their shells – mussels cooked like snails – a plateful could be put in the oven to reheat when needed. They are also tasty breadcrumbed and deep fried with a dip, maybe just tartare or tomato sauce. Shame to lose the glorious mussel stock, though.

Mussels that aren't rope grown can come with barnacles and mud attached, also long unappetising beards that need to be tugged out before cooking. Cleaned mussels will have a much shorter shelf life but involve a lot less effort.

- - - - - - - - - - - - - - - - - - - - - - - - - - - - - - - - - - - - - - - - - - - - - - - - - - - - - - - - - -

2kg mussels – *preferably cleaned: discard any broken ones or those that refuse to close when tapped on the work surface*

300ml white wine

60g butter

100g shallots – *chopped*

1 garlic clove

2 teaspoons curry paste

Pinch of saffron threads

35g plain flour

200ml crème fraîche

1 teaspoon lemon juice

1 tablespoon *chopped* flat-leaf parsley

Salt and freshly ground black pepper

Bring the mussels to the boil with the white wine in a covered saucepan.

In a separate pan, melt the butter and then fry the shallots and garlic. Add the curry paste and saffron, then stir in the flour.

Add the cooking liquor from the mussels one-third at a time, stirring to the boil.

Add the crème fraîche, lemon juice and parsley, then season with salt and pepper.

Mix in the mussels and serve.

# North sea fish soup

### FOR 6

This is a more interesting dish if you manage to assemble four or five different types of fish. The fishmonger should be able to provide the bones and trimmings for the stock. If not, then chicken stock, which is fuller flavoured, will substitute better than commercial fish stock. Bear in mind that denser-textured fish will take longer to cook than fragile specimens. So either cut fish like bass or hake slightly smaller or add them to the stock earlier. The idea is that all the fish should cook to perfection simultaneously. The quantities here are for six starter-sized portions, so scale upwards if you plan it as main course.

200g haddock fillet

200g halibut fillet

200g red mullet fillet

200g sea bass fillet

6 scallops – with corals

18 whole shell-on prawns

50g butter

50ml dry white wine

2 tomatoes

2 slices of white bread

2 shallots – *chopped*

1 teaspoon lemon juice

2 egg yolks

2 tablespoons double cream

2 tablespoons *chopped* flat-leaf parsley

Salt and freshly ground black pepper

Wash the bones and trimmings from the filleted fish, including the scallop corals and the bodies of the prawns. Turn these over with half the butter in a saucepan. When they start to cook, add the wine and 900ml of cold water. Bring to the boil, then simmer for 20 minutes. Turn off the heat, then leave to cool. Strain off the stock – you should have around 600ml.

Skin the tomatoes by dropping them into boiling water, counting to ten, then refreshing them under cold water. The skins will slip off easily. Halve the tomatoes and scoop out the centres. Cut the flesh into dice.

Cut the bread into cubes and fry in the remaining butter until brown. Set aside.

Add the shallots to the stock and bring to the boil.

Cut the fish into large chunks and turn these briefly in lemon juice. Season with salt and black pepper, then drop all, except the prawns, into the simmering stock, scallops last.

Move the pan away from the direct heat. Whisk the egg yolks and cream together in a bowl, then stir this into the stock. Check for seasoning and add salt, black pepper and a little more lemon juice as needed.

Place the tomato, parsley and prawns in a tureen and pour over the soup. Serve with the croutons.

SEA FISH IS WAY SUPERIOR TO FRESHWATER

# FISH SOUPS AND STEWS

The difference between a fish soup and a stew is really the quantity of broth you want in relation to pieces of fish. My preference is for plenty of liquid and a soup spoon to deal with it. If this is your plan also, then remember to spice and season accordingly. A small amount of sauce will have to flavour a large piece of protein, so will need to be stronger and more concentrated.

Fish soups and stews come in every conceivable style. I have used a delicate and lightly flavoured version over the years and called it 'North Sea fish soup'. The general idea is that you taste just-poached chunks of fish with the cooking liquor thickened by a liaison of egg yolk and cream to transform cooking stock into soup. This, with a few spoonfuls of parsley and diced tomato, will be subtle and delicious.

The famous French soups like bouillabaisse are more concerned with the tasty broth than the fish itself and will use spiny fish like rascasse that are more adventure than pleasure to eat. It's the same mindset that likes to negotiate every leaf on a globe artichoke and to take on a whole cooked crab, gladiator style, with crackers and a spoon. Quite understandable of course, and the task will prolong lunch by hours, not to mention give a fascinating cleaning operation on the floor thereafter. With less feeling of achievement but more of enjoyment, I have used only what you actually eat in the recipes on pages 78 and 80.

# Bourride

FOR 6

This is the world's finest fish stew. The fish is braised in saffron stock, then thickened with garlic mayonnaise. As ever, the fish you use will depend on what's available and in top condition. Cheapskates and persons like myself who need to make some form of profit from a dish will also take price and value into consideration. The recipe can be followed in a straight line from soup stock to finished dish. I have set it out the way I make it myself as this gives flexibility on timing and plenty of prep that can be done well in advance. Importantly, it gives you a final opportunity to decide on the strength of the bourride by using all or perhaps slightly less of the soup base in the final assembly of the dish. This is intended to be a main course, but a small serving will make an ideal starter, especially if you are cooking something fairly simple as a main course afterwards, a roast perhaps or grilled things with salad.

As a main course I'd suggest you boil some small waxy potatoes and add them to the broth at the same time as the fish so that they can take on some of the saffron and orange flavours – maybe some poached young leeks as well.

## Garlic mayonnaise

2 egg yolks

3 fat garlic cloves – *crushed*

1 tablespoon Dijon mustard

1 tablespoon lemon juice

50ml olive oil

100ml vegetable oil

Salt and freshly ground black pepper

## Soup base

1 tablespoon vegetable oil

2 shallots – *chopped*

1 garlic clove – *chopped*

1 small red pepper – *deseeded and chopped*

First make the mayonnaise. Whisk together the egg yolks, garlic, mustard, lemon juice and seasonings, then slowly whisk in the oils.

Make the soup base by heating the oil in a large sauce pan and sweating off the shallots, garlic and red pepper until cooked but not coloured. Add the saffron, chilli and orange zest, then the stock or water. Bring this to the boil, then simmer a few minutes. Season with a little salt and black pepper, then liquidise in a blender.

To finish the soup, heat the litre of chicken stock then stir in the base. Sear the red mullet and John Dory fillets – the red mullet skin side only, but a brief searing on both sides for the John Dory – and add them to the pot. The fish will cook very quickly in the hot soup. Lift out into the serving bowls, then at the last moment sear the scallops on both sides and add these too. Liquidise the cooking liquor in a blender, adding the mayonnaise until it is the thickness you want. Maybe add a little more lemon juice and a dash of Tabasco if not spicy enough. Pour over the fish and scallops, and add a few croutons if you fancy.

Large pinch of saffron threads

1 bird's eye chilli – *chopped*

Pared zest from ½ orange

200ml hot chicken stock or water

Salt and freshly ground black pepper

### Fish

1 litre chicken stock

6 red mullet fillets from medium-sized fish

6 x 100g John Dory fillets

6 large scallops

1 teaspoon lemon juice – optional

Tabasco sauce – optional

# Skate with shrimps and dill

FOR 6

Dill, the herb, is astringent but not as aniseed as lookalike fennel. It partners the sweetness of shrimps or crayfish well. A subtle but meaty fish will suit this dish perfectly. So cod or hake would also be fine but not herring, mackerel or red mullet.

Skate is underrated, with firm white flesh and good flavour. The wings do not have any bones as such; the meat sandwiches a layer of bone-like cartilage. Usually this is left in place and, when cooked, the meat is slid down and off it on both sides. This is fine and dandy; however, I prefer to have all skin and cartilage out of the way in advance so that everything on the plate is for eating rather than struggling with. Your fishmonger should, in theory at least, be able to fillet the wings for you in seconds. Should he/she be incompetent or unwilling, you will need to allow 15 minutes in order to do it yourself. Cut away at the flesh on the triangular corner of the wing until you reach the cartilage, then slide a sharp knife, pressing downwards and along the cartilage to release the fillet and repeat for the reverse side of each wing.

6 x 160g skate wing fillets

Olive oil – *for brushing*

**Sauce**

25g unsalted butter

15g plain flour

200ml fish stock or 100ml each white wine and water

½ teaspoon anchovy essence, or 1 anchovy fillet – *finely chopped*

1 teaspoon wholegrain mustard

1 tablespoon crème fraîche

100g *peeled* brown shrimps

25g dill – *chopped*

½ teaspoon lemon juice

A few drops of Tabasco sauce

Salt and freshly ground black pepper

For the sauce, warm the butter in a small saucepan until melted, then stir in the flour to form a soft roux. Let this cook for 1 minute.

Warm the stock or wine/water mix, then stir in one-third of this into the roux. Keep stirring until it boils, more likely forms a slack dough. Add another third and stir this to the boil, then finally repeat the process with the remainder. Strain this into a clean saucepan. The result will make a fine base for the sauce. Whisk in the anchovy, mustard and crème fraîche.

Brush the fillets with the olive oil, then grill on both sides. The fish cooks quite quickly, but the exact timing will depend on the thickness of the fillets – 10–12 minutes is a reasonable guideline.

Add the shrimps and dill to the sauce. Check the seasoning and add salt, black pepper, the lemon juice and Tabasco until it tastes good.

Spoon the sauce onto warm plates and lay the skate on top.

# Pressed salmon with chard and dill pancakes

FOR 6

Pressed salmon – gravadlax – is easy to make. It's also easy to buy providing you buy the best, as is smoked salmon, which would also be fine in this dish. You want top produce prepared by people who understand the point of the process so that you are likely to end up with salmon that tastes more of itself than the smoke.

Pressed salmon is cured with salt. The grav or gravad of its name implies being buried in the ground, but this is a step too far in the search for authenticity – though I did once read a recipe from Paul Bocuse where he advised burying a turkey studded with truffles for some time before digging it up ready to cook. Refrigeration has rendered this sort of caper historic rather than helpful.

The classic accompaniment to pressed salmon is a sweet Swedish mustard sauce with dill. This treatment makes a change. If you have bought ready made and it came with a sachet of this sauce, then you can use a little on the side. Shame to waste anything you have paid for. Most Scandinavian recipes that use peppercorns stipulate the white, stronger, type and the drop of brandy or whisky in the cure strikes me as a very recent addition, so you can leave it out if you prefer. Spirits like cognac or Scotch are vastly more expensive in that part of the world, so would transform this simple fisherman's treat into something expensive and luxurious.

· · · · · · · · · · · · · · · · · · · · · · · · · · · · · · · · · · · · · · · · · · · · · · · · · · · · · · · · · · · · · · · · · · · · · · · ·

1kg salmon fillet – *skin on*

### Cure

4 tablespoons coarse salt

4 tablespoons granulated or demerara sugar

1 bunch of dill – *coarsely chopped*

1 tablespoon *coarsely crushed* white peppercorns

2 tablespoons brandy

Cut the salmon into two equal parts and lay skin-side down on kitchen foil. Mix the cure ingredients and spread over each piece.

Wrap and then put a weight on top. Nothing hugely heavy, a bottle of water perhaps.

Refrigerate for a day, turning the fish over half way through the process.

Scrape off the cure and put the wrapped salmon back in the fridge until needed.

For the pancakes, remove the stems from the chard and boil the leafy parts for 3 minutes. Drain and refresh in iced water for 5 minutes. Squeeze dry and chop finely.

### Pancakes

200g chard

1 whole egg, plus 1 egg white

110g self-raising flour

1 teaspoon baking powder

½ teaspoon salt

1 tablespoon *chopped* dill

150ml whole milk

Olive oil – *for frying*

1 tablespoon crème fraîche per person

Make a batter with the whole egg, flour, baking powder, salt, dill and milk, then stir in the chard.

Separately whisk the extra egg white until stiff, then fold this into the batter.

Warm a little olive oil in a non-stick pan, then pour on 2 tablespoons of batter to make one pancake. Flip when golden and cook for 2 minutes on each side. Repeat until the batter is finished. You can make lots of small pancakes or just half a dozen large ones – I prefer the small pancakes.

Serve the pancakes warm next to slices of pressed salmon with a spoonful of crème fraîche on each plate.

# Smoked haddock and prawn fish pie

This used to be a pub lunch standard before they discovered goat's cheese and rocket salad. It is now poorly made, if ever, with mean fillings of cheap fish. It remains one of my favourite dishes. Lobster will also do nicely if you are short of prawns.

FOR 6

1 kg maincrop potatoes – *peeled and cut into equal sized pieces*

A knob of butter

A little *grated* nutmeg

1 egg yolk

500g undyed smoked haddock fillet

500ml whole milk

30g unsalted butter

25g plain flour

500g large *peeled* prawns

25g *chopped* shallot

25g *chopped* leek

4 hard-boiled eggs – *shelled and cut into quarters*

1 teaspoon mixed spice

½ teaspoon curry powder

1 teaspoon lemon juice

20ml double cream

40g *grated* Cheddar

Zest of ½ lemon

1 tablespoon *chopped* flat-leaf parsley

Salt and freshly ground black pepper

Preheat the oven to 180°C/fan 160°C/gas mark 4.

Boil the potatoes until just cooked, then drain and mash them. Add the butter, nutmeg, salt and pepper and finally the egg yolk.

Cut the haddock into large dice, then poach in the milk.

Cook the unsalted butter and flour into a roux, then stir in one-third of the milk used for poaching. When it's smooth, whisk in the remaining milk, one-third at a time, reboiling until smooth each time. Check the seasoning, then mix in the haddock, prawns, shallot, leek, eggs, spices, lemon and cream.

Pour into a deep baking dish, then pipe or use a spatula to cover with the mashed potato. This is the moment for any decorative work if you want waves or piped twiddly bits on top. Cover with the cheese and lemon zest, then bake for about 30 minutes until crisp and golden. Scatter over the parsley and serve.

# Scallop quenelles

FOR 4

The general rule for this type of lightly poached dish is to have equal volumes, rather than weights, of minced fish to double cream. The mixture is formed into dumplings with the aid of two spoons and slid into simmering water or stock, or it can be shaped into sausages by piping onto clingfilm, which is then wrapped around the fish and tightened before poaching. These sausage shapes are sometimes called 'boudins' or puddings. In either case, test your mixture by poaching a teaspoonful in advance. You will be able to check seasoning as well as texture before it's all too late. The cooked quenelles can be served white straight from the poaching liquor or browned briefly in hot butter. If you prefer the latter, then I find the sausage-shaped quenelles work better.

I have never used the corals on scallops, which is possibly a waste. The Capital Hotel when I was there used a similar mixture and method to make a scallop terrine, which combined hake and scallop. The corals were prepared separately with a touch less cream and piped along the middle so that the finished dish, when cooked, chilled and served alongside horseradish cream and, for some reason, redcurrant jelly, looked like the Japanese flag.

The mixture needs to be chilled throughout, so try not to overwork the processing and maybe add the cream over a bowl of iced water.

........................................................................

150g white scallop meat

100g white fish fillet – sole or halibut for preference

1 large egg white

A little *grated* nutmeg

150ml double cream

Salt and freshly ground black pepper

Put the fish in a food processor with the egg white and a pinch each of nutmeg, salt and pepper. Purée until smooth, then scrape out and into a bowl.

Work in the cream with a spatula. Check the seasoning, then cover with clingfilm and refrigerate for 2 hours.

If you are using spoons, then dip both into warm water. Take a scoop with one spoon, then scrape it into the other spoon, back and forth until you have a smooth, neat oval. Drop in a pan of simmering salted water until done. The timing will depend on the size of the quenelles, but 8–12 minutes is a good guide and they will feel firm to the touch. Lift onto kitchen paper to drain.

If you want boudin shapes, then pipe the mixture along clingfilm, wrap tightly and refrigerate for 1 hour before poaching for about the same time. These parcels will need to be warmed in hot water then unwrapped, of course, before sliding into foaming butter to be browned.

# Confit salmon

FOR 4

Confit is an overused word, often just describing anything cooked in fat. It originally described the method of cooking and preserving goose or duck legs and involves salting or lightly curing, then slow cooking in goose or duck fat. It's a fabulous method of keeping the flesh soft during long cooking. The same principle can be used for other meats and fish, and even the fat that defines it can be substituted for warm to quite hot olive oil. It's easy enough, a bit like slow-speed deep-frying, and suits fish like salmon. I have used olive oil to cook small birds like quail with this method, but prefer goose fat. Hot olive oil in any case would need to be the cheapest – products like pomace, which represents the final boiling up of the olives for one last pressing – or it will be a waste of money.

4 x 150g salmon fillets – *preferably skinned*

2 teaspoons coarse salt

1 teaspoon coarsely ground black pepper

1 teaspoon granulated sugar

750ml goose fat

Mix the salt, black pepper and sugar together, then sprinkle over the salmon fillets. Cover with clingfilm and leave in the fridge for 30 minutes. Wash and pat the fish dry with kitchen paper.

Warm the fat in a large saucepan to about 40°C if you have a thermometer – or until it's becoming uncomfortable to stick your finger in. So that's rather warm but nowhere near chip-frying temperatures. The idea is slow and gentle cooking rather than frying. Slip the salmon into the fat: 15 minutes will do the trick over a gentle heat. A lot depends on the thickness of the salmon fillets and how much you have lowered the temperature by adding lots of fish to the pan at once, but of course underdone salmon will be okay and the fish can be heated quickly under a grill if you prefer a hot result.

# Watercress and horseradish cream

Remember the inevitable grilled tomato and sprig of hairy watercress that partnered all mixed grills and steak back in the day? Watercress was wasted as garnish for it has a powerful and assertive flavour. People who like watercress will usually be fond of ingredients like mustard, radishes and horseradish. And those who don't will not be trying this recipe.

SERVES 6

1 bunch of watercress

1 teaspoon Dijon mustard

1 tablespoon horseradish cream

1 tablespoon soured cream

100ml double cream

Squeeze of lemon juice

Salt

Pick over the watercress and roughly chop. Whisk the mustard, horseradish and soured cream together, then add the cream, watercress and a pinch of salt.

Add the lemon juice, then whisk until the cream forms peaks.

Serve a spoonful beside each salmon fillet.

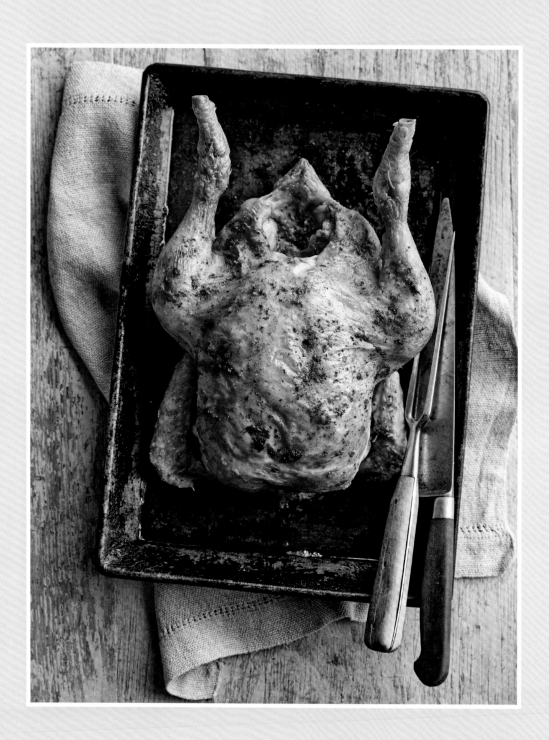

# MOST POULTRY IS TASTELESS

The transformation of chicken from celebratory treat to everyday meat has not come without drawbacks. Quality has declined and chicken has lost some of its allure, in fact acquiring new status as junk food alongside burgers. Interestingly, battery-farmed chicken is the greenest, most environmentally friendly meat because a great proportion of the feed used turns directly into meat. Good news for the planet and the wallet perhaps, but not so clever for the chicken. There is better news as well, though, for those producing proper chicken. Free-range and decently fed birds are being marketed and sold at the right quality and price by smart shops and supermarkets, a system that the French recognised as the way forward long ago, and one that puts a premium on the variety of bird, how long it lived and what it was fed. It's not just that you can now pay quite a lot for good chicken, it's that those who produce better birds will see some reward for their efforts and some justification in spending extra money and resources on their crop.

> All meat should be a special treat and not necessarily an everyday ingredient

It can seem snobbish to complain about cheap meat. There are still plenty of people who live on tight food budgets. But all meat should be a special treat and not necessarily an everyday ingredient. We should be able to feel good about the product and the conditions in which fellow creatures were raised.

Not all poultry is chicken of course. Birds like quail, turkey and guinea fowl are available and provide differing textures and tastes. Similarly the duck family – domesticated varieties like Aylesbury, which are derived from the Chinese Peking type, and newer, slightly more mallard-like ducks such as Gressingham.

## HANDLING

Raw poultry carries high levels of bacteria, so safe storage and preparation are important. Never wash the bird because you will splash bacteria around your sink and work surfaces. Scrub the board and knives you use in hot soapy water before using them again and definitely before carving the cooked bird. Store raw poultry on the bottom shelf of the fridge so that any juices that may escape don't drip onto other food.

Some poultry – chicken and guinea fowl, for instance – have little fat covering and are prone to dry out quickly unless covered with either clingfilm or a fine coating of oil. If you plan to freeze the bird, then double-wrap beforehand. In general, poultry that has been bought fresh then frozen at home will have more flavour despite all the advanced quick-freezing techniques. Commercially prepared birds are frozen within a very short time of their slaughter and before they have had time to develop their own natural flavour in the same way that game birds and meat carcasses do when hung.

## PREPARING

A fresh bird should have no dry patches on the skin. These indicate poor storage and will need lots of extra butter, fat or oil to mitigate this during cooking. Poultry is often sold trussed, that is tied up with string so that it looks plumper and tidier. This doesn't help during cooking as it makes the penetration of heat less even and involves the removal of all this string before any carving and eating is possible. So untruss your bird.

Lastly all birds have a wishbone, the arched bone that surrounds the neck cavity. It's best to cut this away before cooking. It does no harm to the meat of course, but makes carving difficult once cooked as it is embedded in the thickest part of the breast meat.

## POULTRY SECTIONS

There are two main parts: the breasts and the legs. Winglets can be left attached to the breasts or separated if wished. The leg meat is darker and denser in texture than the pale breast meat and takes a little longer to cook. Swift cooking processes such as frying or grilling work well with breast meat, and slow processes like braising and poaching are best with the dark meat. You can compensate for this when roasting or poaching a whole bird by placing it on its side while cooking or, even better, roast it breast-side down. You'll need to turn the bird over during the cooking, of course – so that each leg will have taken the brunt of the heat if the bird was cooked on its side, or so that the breast can gain an attractive colour if you cooked it face down.

## ROASTING GRAVY

The tin that you use for roasting will have residues of the meat juices and small caramelised pieces of meat attached. These are concentrate and provide better flavour than any stock cube. They just need to be revived with water or a combination of water and wine. It doesn't take long, about the time the bird should rest before carving. You can of course jazz things up with fresh herbs or garlic, and you can add a few drops of cream if you want to turn the result into a sauce, or a few drops of vinegar if you want to turn it into a dressing for, say, a roast quail that is to be served as the hot component of a warm salad.

Skim off the fat – it will rise naturally on top of the pan juices. Put the roasting tin over a low heat and mix a tablespoon of plain flour with the same amount of skimmed fat. Wheat flour gives a much better texture than cornflour or even potato flour. Pour in an appropriate amount of wine or water, about 300ml for a roast chicken, and a tablespoon of tomato passata. Bring to the boil, then whisk in the fat and flour mixture. Bring this to the boil again, skim off any foam or fat that rises to the surface, then strain into a clean saucepan or gravy boat.

## STUFFINGS

It's traditional to make a roast bird more interesting with a stuffing. Stuffing doesn't have to be stuffed anywhere of course, least of all in the main cavity where it gets little heat and may well be uncooked by the time everything else is ready, especially if meat is involved. Some people work the stuffing between the skin and breast. This works fine but, to my mind, makes the bird look as if it had some nasty affliction. Presumably the object is to incorporate any juices from the bird into the flavour. I prefer to cook the stuffing separately, although in the same tray if there is room. Most stuffings are a mix of dried fruit and herbs alongside fresh breadcrumbs to sop up the moisture. I like apricot, watercress and hazelnuts mixed into the crumbs, also diced apples, pears and chestnuts with lots of spices and some sausage meat mixed into the crumbs. The choice is yours.

# Roast goose with red cabbage

FOR 6

Geese are smart enough to be impossible to rear intensively so are always free range and consequently always expensive. I eat goose rather than turkey at Christmas because it is such a rare treat, whereas you can eat a turkey any time. Also, because the crisp skin is so delicious and there is comparatively little meat per kilo of goose there will be fewer leftovers to negotiate if people weren't as hungry as you expected.

You will have giblets with the goose and very little to make gravy with after roasting. Bring the giblets to the boil in 2 litres of water and throw in a diced onion. Simmer for at least an hour, by which time it will have reduced and you will have around 1 litre of stock. Strain this into a jug and, when you have roasted your goose and decanted its excellent fat into a container, you can pour this stock into the roasting tray to make the gravy.

---

1 x 5kg goose – *giblets removed*

1 small red cabbage

½ bottle cheap red wine

Juice of 2 oranges

1 tablespoon sugar

1 teaspoon mixed spice

Salt and freshly ground black pepper

Preheat the oven to 200°C/fan 180°C/gas mark 6.

Prick the goose all over so that the fat can escape during cooking. Wrap the legs in foil, then place on its back in a large roasting tray. Add 2 tablespoons of water. Roast the goose for 2½ hours.

While the goose roasts, thinly slice the cabbage then marinate it for 1 hour in the red wine and orange juice in a heavy-bottomed pan. Season with the sugar, salt, black pepper and spice, then bring to the boil. Cover with a lid and simmer for 20 minutes. It won't come to any harm if you then switch off the heat until you are ready to reheat and serve with the goose.

After the goose has cooked for 1 hour, turn it breast-side down then, 30 minutes later, remove the foil from the legs and turn the bird onto its back once more. Pour the accumulated fat into a container. You can use this to roast potatoes. If the skin is not crisp enough you can sprinkle a little flour over it.

Like all bird and meat joints, the goose is best when rested for 20 minutes. Carve the cooked bird in the same way you would a duck. Cut away each leg then, assuming you have removed the wishbone, it will be easy to cut off each cooked breast. The legs can be divided into thighs and drumsticks, and the breasts cut into as many pieces as you wish. Goose is best served well done so you won't carve long elegant slices, rather a filleted piece or two per person.

# Coq au vin

FOR 4

This is a staple of the French provincial repertoire. It's also regularly one of the worst-cooked brasserie dishes. Sometimes the chicken pieces are marinated overnight to deepen the effect of the red wine. This will darken the chicken and has the side effect of drying it out as well as overpowering any chicken flavour the bird has to contribute.

Unlike braised lamb or beef, coq au vin does not reheat well but compensates by giving a freshness and vitality many other braised dishes cannot. The process favours leg and thigh meat over breast. It's cheaper and easier to buy thighs and drumsticks separately than it is to buy a whole chicken and dismantle it.

There are lots of variations on this dish; white wine instead of red will produce something that is very different but also excellent. In the days of imitation-Escoffier cuisine in posh restaurants, I recall making one called 'poulet sauté Marengo', named after one of Napoleon's successful battles, as was his favourite horse. This called for a deep-fried egg to be served on top of the braised chicken. A specific herb – oregano or basil perhaps – added right at the end will also add a nuance of flavour. Use a decent wine – a cheaper Burgundy would be ideal.

· · · · · · · · · · · · · · · · · · · · · · · · · · · · · · · · · · · · · · · · · · · · · · · · · · · · · · · · · · · · · · · · · · · · · · · · · · · · · · ·

12 chicken thighs

50g unsalted butter

8 small pickling onions

100g lardons

16 button mushrooms

2 garlic cloves – *crushed*

1 tablespoon plain flour

1 tablespoon tomato passata

250ml red wine

1 teaspoon sugar

300ml chicken stock or water

2 tablespoons *chopped* flat-leaf parsley

Salt and freshly ground black pepper

Season the chicken with salt and black pepper.

Heat half the butter in a heavy-based saucepan, then brown the chicken on each side.

Add the onions, lardons and mushrooms, and let these also colour and cook for 10 minutes before adding the garlic.

Stir in the flour to combine with the coloured butter and cooking juices. Add the passata, then the red wine and sugar.

Add the stock or water. Bring to the boil, then immediately lower the heat to the barest simmer. Cover and cook gently for about 25 minutes until the chicken is tender.

Lift out the meat and the vegetables into a warm serving dish.

Pour all the cooking liquor into a liquidiser and blend, adding the remaining butter. You will need to do this in a couple of batches. Test for seasoning, then pour over the chicken. Sprinkle with the parsley and garnish with heart-shaped croutons.

# Spiced quails in salad

This dish looks complex but is straightforward and not reliant on any reduced stocks or preparations of the commercial kitchen. Most dishes of a Middle Eastern nature seem to assume a healthily stocked store cupboard, but the only piece of kit that is necessary will be a liquidiser for the dressing.

FOR 4

4 large quails

**Marinade**

½ small red pepper

½ small chilli

1 large garlic clove –*peeled*

1 tablespoon *chopped* fresh mint

1 teaspoon ground cumin

1 teaspoon saffron threads

2 tablespoons olive oil

Salt and freshly ground black pepper

**Dressing**

2 tablespoons water

2 tablespoons olive oil

1 teaspoon sesame oil

1 tablespoon pine kernels – *not toasted*

1 tablespoon *chopped* flat-leaf parsley

A few drops each lemon juice, soy sauce and Tabasco sauce

**Salad**

Mixed salad leaves

1 teaspoon olive oil

A few drops of lemon juice

A few pomegranate seeds

1 tablespoon pine kernels – *toasted*

Chop the marinade ingredients together and crush them to a pulp with the flat of a knife or a mortar and pestle. Work in the olive oil, then massage the result over the quails. Leave for 2 hours or overnight.

Preheat the oven to 180°C/fan 160°C/gas mark 4. Roast the quails for about 20 minutes until done.

To make the dressing, put all the ingredients into a liquidiser and blend to a smooth dressing. Your aim is for the consistency of double cream, so add a little extra oil if too thin or a little extra water if too thick.

When the quails are done, dress the salad leaves lightly with the olive oil, lemon and some salt. Place this onto cold plates. Trickle the dressing around the salad, scatter with the pomegranate seeds and pine kernels and place the quails on top. Deglaze the roasting tin with a little water and spoon this onto each quail.

## MARINADES

Marinades come in two types: wine or vinegar ones tend to be stronger and will dry out whatever is left in them, whereas oil marinades will have less impact but tend to moisten whatever is left in them. I have used plenty of oil marinades that also have spices like cinnamon or even chilli, but am not sure how much extra flavour these really give. It's the residues of the chilli oil or the cinnamon and orange zest still clinging to the outside of the meat with the oil that affect things, and these can be added at any time.

# Guinea fowl with lentils and sage

The idea here is that the breasts are grilled and the legs braised. The breasts will need to be batted out lightly to even out the thickness and tenderise the meat. It's then seasoned with pepper and brushed with plenty of olive oil as a sort of marinade.

Guinea fowl legs are best braised. This gives an opportunity for producing a well-flavoured stock as part of the finished dish. Here it brings depth to a braised lentil accompaniment.

FOR 4

· · · · · · · · · · · · · · · · · · · · · · · · · · · · · · · · · · · · · · · · · · · · · · ·

2 guinea fowl

Olive oil

1 litre chicken stock

1 onion – *chopped*

1 stick of celery – *peeled and chopped*

1 leek – *washed and chopped*

1 carrot – *peeled and cut into fine dice*

1 garlic clove – *chopped*

2 rashers of streaky bacon – *cut into strips*

240g tin green or brown lentils – *drained*

175ml white wine

Vegetable oil – *for frying*

8 sage leaves

Salt and freshly ground black pepper

Preheat the oven to 160°C/fan 140°C/gas mark 3.

Remove the skin from the guinea fowl crown. Cut out the wishbones, then carefully remove each breast fillet. Pull back the legs and cut these away. Cut the carcasses into small pieces.

Place each breast between two sheets of clingfilm and flatten slightly so that they are approximately equal thickness. Season with black pepper, then brush generously with olive oil and keep in the fridge until needed.

Heat a little oil in a pan, sear the legs and carcass bones until brown, then transfer to a roasting tin. Cover with the stock then with kitchen foil across the roasting tin. Bring to the boil then transfer to the oven and cook until completely tender. Test the meat after 1 hour but leave for longer if not soft. Lift out the legs, then scrape the meat into a dish for later. Strain the stock into a jug; you should have about 500ml.

Fry the vegetables and bacon, add the lentils, wine and reserved stock and let cook gently until most of the stock has evaporated and the lentils are a porridge-like consistency. Stir in the leg meat.

Grill the breasts. Timing will depend on their thickness and the heat – ten minutes should be plenty. You want them to be tender.

Deep-fry the sage leaves. The oil used won't be good for much afterwards, so do this in a frying pan generously filled to a depth of 1 cm, then lift out the leaves onto kitchen paper as they crisp.

Serve the breast on a bed of the braised lentils and leg meat, then scatter the sage leaves on top.

# Chicken tikka

FOR 4

This staple of the Indian takeaway will surprise you. A yogurt marinade alters the texture as well as the flavour and will need a few hours to do the job properly. Drink a glass of Riesling or Gewurztraminer with it rather than lager to complete the contrast. The bright red colouring of tandoori chicken is not required.

. . . . . . . . . . . . . . . . . . . . . . . . . . . . . . . . . . . . . . . . . . . . . . . . . . . . . . . . . . . . . . . . .

4 large skinless chicken breasts

25g butter

**Marinade**

150g Greek-style yogurt

1 tablespoon *peeled, chopped and crushed* fresh ginger

1 large garlic clove – *crushed*

½ small chilli, *chopped*

1 teaspoon ground cinnamon

1 teaspoon ground cumin

1 teaspoon cardamom seeds, *crushed*

1 tablespoon lemon juice

Salt

The chicken breasts cook better with the bones attached – they stretch the meat as it cooks. Not the end of the world if you can only buy them ready filleted. They will cook more quickly, of course, but tend to curl up at their point.

Mix all the marinade ingredients together and coat the chicken breasts with the result. Cover and leave for a few hours in the fridge.

Dot the chicken with the butter and grill until done. This should take about 30 minutes and can also be done in a preheated oven (200°C/fan 180°C/gas mark 6) or some combination of the two.

Serve with wedges of lemon or lime and a raita dip.

## RAITA

100g Greek-style yogurt

1 teaspoon cumin seeds – *toasted and crushed*

1 tablespoon *chopped* mint

1 tablespoon cucumber – *cut into small dice*

Salt

Whisk everything together and serve separately.

# Poached chicken pot au feu with summer herbs and vegetables

FOR 4

White meat like chicken is excellent poached. The trick is merely patience and a suitably sized saucepan. The faster you try to cook the chicken, the drier and drearier it will be. We are not talking Heston Blumenthal's 24-hour slow cooking here, an hour max will be plenty. But at no point should any boiled meat actually boil. A slight simmer will deliver a soft texture and retain all the flavour with the bonus of the cooking liquor to use as either part of the dish, as soup or as an asset in the freezer for another day.

The chicken is best if covered by liquid. A lid will ensure that anything poking out from its stock will still cook but make it more difficult to notice when the temperature rises above what's needed.

The sauce is a version of hollandaise made using the cooking liquor and finished with a little tangy crème fraîche.

1.5kg whole chicken

12 small new potatoes

100g runner beans – *stringed and sliced*

100g broad beans – *shelled and podded*

4 baby courgettes – *part-peeled and halved lengthways*

50g peas, fresh or frozen

3 egg yolks

100g unsalted butter – *melted then heated*

1 tablespoon each *chopped* flat-leaf parsley, *snipped* chives and basil

1 teaspoon lemon juice

A few drops of Tabasco sauce

1 tablespoon crème fraîche

Salt

Measure just enough water to cover the bird in a large pot and bring this to the boil. Add the potatoes then the chicken. Gently simmer until done. The chicken will be completely cooked in 40 minutes, the potatoes may take a little longer, depending on their size. If you pierce the bird through the thighs, which take longest, the juices should flow clear rather than bloody.

Lift the chicken from the pot. Do this carefully, tipping the bird so that the cavity juice empties back into the pot rather than over your hands and work surface. Bring the liquor to the boil, then add the vegetables in the order in which they take to cook: runner beans first, then broad beans, finally courgettes and peas.

Whilst the vegetables are cooking, lift out two spoonfuls of the cooking liquor and whisk this with the yolks over the boiling liquid, a bowl that fits snugly over the pot is an advantage. The idea is that this cooks into a sabayon, much like beginning a hollandaise sauce.

Away from the heat, whisk in the melted butter, then add the herbs, lemon juice, Tabasco, crème fraîche and salt.

Carve the chicken and divide between four deep dishes or large soup bowls. Spoon on the vegetables and cooking liquor, and serve with the sauce separate. You'll need a spoon for the stock as well as a knife and fork.

# Southern fried chicken

FOR 4

This recipe has more in common with chicken tikka than you might suppose. Buttermilk acts on the chicken much in the way yogurt does, so that the result tastes quite different from chicken merely crumbed and fried. You can adapt your fried chicken to suit your taste by adding whatever herbs you most like. The late Colonel Sanders evidently had a secret eleven herbs and spices in his world-conquering recipe. Shame the chicken that's used isn't better.

2 boneless chicken breasts

2 boneless chicken thighs

1 teaspoon freshly ground black pepper

1 level teaspoon salt

Good pinch of cayenne pepper

1 tablespoon Dijon mustard

150ml buttermilk

Vegetable oil – *for frying*

4 rashers of bacon

150g fresh breadcrumbs

Slice each breast and thigh into four. Mix the seasonings and mustard together, then brush this over the pieces of chicken.

Put the chicken pieces into a bowl and pour over the buttermilk. Turn the pieces so that they are all coated. Let this marinate for 30 minutes.

Heat a pan with a little oil, then fry the bacon until crisp. As soon as it's cool enough to handle, crumble into small pieces and mix with the breadcrumbs. Coat the chicken with these crumbs.

Add more oil to the pan, about a depth of 1cm is ideal, and fry the chicken pieces for 7–10 minutes until golden brown. You may need to do this in batches, if so strain the oil between each batch so that burnt crumbs don't spoil the following pieces and top up the oil as required. The oil temperature is important: too cool and the chicken will absorb oil rather than fry; too hot, starting to smoke perhaps, and the coating will be brown before the chicken is cooked. If in any doubt, cut open a piece and check – the meat should not be at all pink. A hot oven will finish them off if needed.

Serve with coleslaw.

# Lemon chicken with green olives

FOR 4

Lemon and chicken go well together. In the Maghreb region of North Africa chicken braised with salted (preserved) lemon is a standard dish, and lots of people, myself included, will put a whole lemon in the central cavity of a bird to be roasted. You can chargrill the chicken rather than roast it as here if you prefer the barbecue scorch marks and a faster result.

Another good way of producing lemon flavour is to pare off the rind and cut it into fine strips. Macerate these in the lemon's juice for an hour, then drain and crisp-fry in hot oil. The strips cook in seconds, so use a couple of small frying pans, one with hot oil and the other ready to take the drained oil afterwards. Fry, then pour oil and lemon straight into a sieve. You'll have intensely lemony strips to scatter across the finished dish and a lemon-scented oil for cooking.

4 chicken breasts

50g unsalted butter

16 pitted green olives

2 tablespoons *chopped* flat-leaf parsley

**For the marinade**

4 tablespoons olive oil

1 lemon, *grated* rind and juice

2 garlic cloves, *crushed*

A few thyme leaves (½ teaspoonful)

½ teaspoon ground cumin

Salt and coarsely ground black pepper

Mix the marinade ingredients together. Rub over the chicken. Cover and leave to marinate for 2 hours in the fridge. Turn the chicken from time to time.

Preheat the oven to 160°C/fan 140°C/gas mark 3. Butter an ovenproof baking dish, then put in the chicken and its marinade. Dot the remaining butter on top.

Roast for about 20 minutes until tender and just cooked through, turning and basting the chicken regularly. Halve the olives and add these.

Sprinkle with the parsley and serve.

## KNIVES

Sharp knives are important for most cookery and you can buy knives that are designed for specific tasks. Boning knives are held dagger style so the power is directed downwards and into the joint. Cooks' knives are wide at the handle tapering down to a point, so that you can chop onions or whatever with your fingers crimped against the blade without losing any in the process. Blunt knives will need a sharpening stone but are really best ground by a butcher who will have the right equipment. Light honing of a knife that is losing its edge but not completely blunt can be done with a steel. Place the pointed end of the steel firmly against a cutting board that has kitchen paper or a cloth between it and the work surface to keep it steady, then draw the knife towards the board and away from yourself at an angle of 45 degrees, exerting as much pressure as is safe. Repeat the process with the other knife edge until it's as sharp as you need.

# Spatchcocked poussins

FOR 4

Poussin is French for a baby chicken. I'm reluctant to use French when there are perfectly fine English words available. However, I'm not sure about how appetising terms like 'baby' are when used for meat rather than courgettes or carrots. In fact, very young creatures used for meat tend to be under flavoured, a trade-off for being more tender.

Poussins are best spatchcocked, what the French describe as 'en crapaudine' – in the shape of a toad. You can buy them ready butchered in this style but it's easy enough to do the job yourself. Take out the wishbone, place the bird breast-down on a cutting board, then cut out the spine. A pair of kitchen scissors will do the trick. Press the chicken flat and if necessary crack the central breastbone to make it easier.

Dry cider is a versatile ingredient, used much as dry white wine but of course giving a slightly different flavour. Bit cheaper though usually, if that's a help.

The poussins are scored three or four times on the flesh side to allow the mustard to seep in, and also to ensure the bird isn't pulled out of shape as the meat cooks and contracts.

· · · · · · · · · · · · · · · · · · · · · · · · · · · · · · · · · · · · · · · · · · · · · · · · · · · · · · · · · · · ·

4 poussins – *spatchcocked*

1 tablespoon olive oil

2 tablespoons Dijon mustard

100ml dry cider

8 ready-to-eat prunes – firm pruneaux d'Agen style

2 tablespoons crème fraîche

25g unsalted butter

Salt and freshly ground black pepper

Preheat the oven to 180°C/fan 160°C/gas mark 4.

Season the poussins and brush them with the olive oil. Sear briefly on each side and transfer to a roasting tin.

Slacken the mustard with 1 tablespoon of the cider, then brush this over the meat side of the birds.

Roast these with the prunes alongside for about 20 minutes until done. Prick with a sharp knife and if the juices run clear the birds are done.

Lift out the poussins and deglaze the roasting tin with the cider. Put the tin over a moderate heat and let it bubble and reduce. Stir in the crème fraîche, then the butter, to thicken the sauce. Serve each poussin next to a small pool of sauce.

# 6

HUNTERS PAY MORE FOR THE

# EXCITEMENT

## OF SHOOTING GAME BIRDS

## THAN SHOPPERS DO FOR THE

# PLEASURE

### OF EATING THEM

# Just because you can eat it doesn't mean you have to.

Autumn is the start of the game bird season, barring a few expensive early grouse, of course. Best of all, in the UK, native flat oysters are back on the menu. Oysters are not classified as game, of course, but flat natives are really as much a wild autumn treat as venison. With luck the weather will have mellowed but not yet seriously deteriorated. Much more than summer, this is the time for those who love cooking and eating.

Game birds represent great value. They are free range even if some species like partridge and pheasant are barely wild. They are well fed and looked after. Until they are shot, of course. This may be a mediocre prospect for the partridge, but is the price to pay for all the earlier nurturing and free space to roam. Hunters pay more per bird for the excitement of shooting them than shoppers do for the pleasure of eating them. If only abattoirs could come to the same arrangement an era of cheaper meat could be in prospect. In any case, it's an anomaly that suits me fine.

Grouse has uniquely flavoured meat, not to everyone's taste because it is powerful and gamey. Partridge and pheasant are white-fleshed like chicken but nowhere near as innocuous. Both have tendencies towards dryness when roasted and I have always found that lots of extra fat, either butter or oil, smeared over the bird helps keep it tender. Turning the bird as it cooks and then using a spoon to baste will also ensure juicy meat. Woodcock and snipe are evidently difficult to shoot – hence the word sniper for an ace marksman. They also crap automatically on take off. Traditionally, woodcock and snipe have been cooked intact, guts in and head on. The brains are a tiny morsel and eaten like a lollipop. I am less enamoured of the lukewarm insides smeared over toast. Just because you can eat it doesn't mean you have to.

A word on cooking any game birds. These creatures have evolved for running about in woodlands or flying across fields. The ability to cook evenly throughout the carcass has not been a factor. Some are good roasted whole, grouse and woodcock for example, but most aren't. The legs will be tougher and more sinewy so that the breasts on a crown of partridge or mallard will be overcooked long before the legs are approaching edible. The solution is to cook them separately. Cut off the pheasant or partridge legs and sear them until brown. Add enough stock, water, wine or a mixture of the three to cover. Top with a lid or kitchen foil and cook in a moderate oven for about 1½–2 hours (160°C/fan 140°C/gas mark 3) until completely tender. The cooking liquor will, with minimal help, give you an excellent sauce or gravy for the finished dish.

## SHUCKING OYSTERS

There are two main types of oyster: natives, which are flat and only available during autumn and winter; and rock oysters, which are deeper, slightly less fine for eating raw, and notionally at least available year round.

Oyster beds are monitored for pollution, but the odd rogue oyster will still appear. One Christmas I treated the family to 100 superb-looking native oysters from one of the most respected sources in Ireland, only to have the holiday ruined for the unlucky member who downed a bad one. Always smell an oyster before popping it in your mouth: it should have a delicate aroma of the sea and nothing more.

- Wash the oysters before you start. Then fold a tea towel so that you can hold the shell tightly and safely while opening.

- Place the oyster, curved-side downwards and with the hinge of its triangular shape outwards, onto the folded tea towel.

- Hold the shell firmly down and then poke the blade of the oyster knife into the hinge. Twist then lift the flat shell away. The difficult part is done.

- Cut the oyster loose from its shell. If there is any debris, then wash the oyster before replacing it.

- Oysters that are intended to be eaten raw are best when just opened, so don't do this too far in advance or you will find they leak out quite a bit of juice.

## DRESSING

You can eat oysters with just a few drops of lemon and Tabasco sauce – I prefer the green version, made with jalapeño, which is more citric and slightly less powerful. Otherwise, a small ramekin of wine vinegar with chopped shallots, salt and black pepper – no oil – is fine. Some people like a few shavings of horseradish or some Worcestershire sauce as well. Serve oysters that are to be eaten raw as cold as possible, preferably on crushed ice.

# Warm rock oysters with spring onion butter sauce

Rock oysters are good served warm; natives would be a waste of their extra cost.

FOR 4

. . . . . . . . . . . . . . . . . . . . . . . . . . . . . . . . . . . . . . . . . . . . . . . . . . . . . . . . . . . . . . . . . . . . . . . . . .

2 dozen oysters

100ml white wine

1 shallot– *chopped*

500g unsalted butter

1 tablespoon crème fraîche

Juice of 1 lemon

Salt, freshly ground black pepper and Tabasco sauce

6 spring onions – *finely sliced*

Shuck the oysters (see page 109). Boil the shells and keep the molluscs in a bowl in a cold place until needed. You'll find that they produce a fair amount of liquid after a short time.

Heat the white wine and shallot, then whisk in the butter, a knob at a time. Finish with the crème fraîche and season with the lemon juice, salt, black pepper and Tabasco. Add the spring onions and a little of the oyster juices last of all.

Arrange six hot shells on each plate, then slide an oyster into each. Spoon the warm butter sauce over top then serve.

The combination of hot shell and warm sauce will heat the oysters as much as needed. A teaspoon of salmon eggs or caviar on each oyster at the final moment is rather fine and will transform the dish into something majestic.

HUNTERS PAY MORE FOR THE EXCITEMENT OF SHOOTING...

# Oyster fritters

MAKES ENOUGH BATTER FOR
2 DOZEN OYSTERS

Again, rock oysters are fine for this dish. You can serve an oyster fritter on top of a poached or grilled piece of white fish to give contrast, or with a salad of autumn leaves and some fried bacon pieces. The batter has Guinness. In fact, I have never been able to detect much of the beer flavour once everything has been added, stirred, then deep fried. However, there is only a small amount called for and I am partial to a drop of chilled stout to deal with the leftovers from the can. You could substitute water, and in fact you could buy tempura batter mix from an oriental supermarket and that would work well also.

· · · · · · · · · · · · · · · · · · · · · · · · · · · · · · · · · · · · · · · · · · · · · · · · · · · · · · · · · · · · · · · · · · · · · · · · · · · · · ·

**Batter**

150ml *chilled* draught Guinness
or Murphy's, or water

125g self-raising flour

Salt

1 tablespoon olive oil

2 egg whites

Mix all the ingredients, except the egg whites, to a smooth paste. Whisk the egg whites until stiff, then fold them in.

Dip the shucked oysters into the batter, then deep-fry until crisp and golden. This is best achieved by frying the oysters a couple at a time. Too many at once will reduce the oil temperature and leave you a soggy rather than crisp finish.

## WILD DUCK

The main types of duck on offer will be mallard, the slightly smaller widgeon and the quail-sized teal. All taste fairly similar and the cooking method merely requires a little common sense in scaling down the timings.

The garnish or herb you use to define this dish is immaterial compared to the care with which you prepare and cook the duck. Roasting and braising liquor will provide a sauce that you can jazz up with some wild mushrooms, truffles or spice mixture.

Mallards yield a generous portion for one, too much for me in fact, but a rather tight portion for two. If you are eating one course only, then a mallard per person is fine. Otherwise one big bird divided between two will be enough.

HUNTERS PAY MORE FOR THE EXCITEMENT OF SHOOTING...

The legs are full of flavour but sinewy. If you cook the bird whole the tendons in the legs will floss your teeth if underdone. Best to cut the legs away and braise them slowly for a couple of hours, then roast the crown – that's the two breasts conjoined on a small base of backbone – 30 minutes before eating.

Prepare the mallards as follows:

Cut the legs free. Discard the wings, or use them to make a stock. Snap away the front of the spine. It will break naturally at the half-way stage. Cut away the wishbone. Lift the flap of skin that covers the neck cavity, then cut around the arch so that the wishbone is free. This makes carving easier once the bird is cooked. Brush the crown with oil.

Cook the birds as follows:

Braise the legs. Brown in an ovenproof pan in oil, then add water, stock or wine. Cover with a lid or kitchen foil, then place in the oven at 170°C/fan 150°C/gas mark 3 to slowly braise. When the legs are melting soft, in probably around 2 hours' time, remove from the oven. Sear the crown of duck so that the skin is browned. Roast at 180°C/fan 160°C/gas mark 4 for 15 minutes, then remove from the oven. The meat will be very rare but don't take fright. Carve away the breasts from either side of the crown. This is easily achieved by cutting straight down each side of the breastbone. Lay the breasts – which will still be blue – in the roasting tin and return to the oven for a further 5 minutes.

Serve the birds as follows:

The legs are easy. Just reheat in the braising liquor, which, strained and skimmed, will make a good sauce. Carve the breasts. Hold the breasts still and firm with an upturned carving fork – the idea is to hold the meat steady while you slice – then carve lengthways, top to bottom not across the middle, into three or four long, thin slices.

The carving is as important as the cooking. Rare wild duck is only tender when cut thin – think salami or prosciutto. Similarly, if you cut across the breast rather than along its length you will either have thick, tough, slices or lots of thin slices that will be cold before you have the chance to serve them.

# WILD DUCK WITH MORELS

Cook the birds as described but add red wine and dried morels to the braising liquor. Dried morels can be dusty and contain sand or grit, so soak them in water and when soft enough split in half before use. They impart bags of flavour but have no texture worth saving, so chop them up as you wish. Midway through cooking the legs, sprinkle a heaped teaspoon of plain flour onto the liquor and stir this in. It will thicken the final sauce and make it less greasy.

# Wild duck with passion fruit

Generally, I'm not a fan of fruit and meat combinations. The passion fruit here though is quite sharp and cuts through the richness of the meat, providing a contrast to that and to the pan juices that derive from the braised legs.

FOR 4

· · · · · · · · · · · · · · · · · · · · · · · · · · · · · · · · · · · · · · · · · · · · · · · · · · · · · · · · · · · · · · · · · · · · · · · · · · · · · · · · · ·

4 mallards

A little sunflower oil –
*for frying*

1 tablespoon plain flour

25ml red wine

500ml stock or water

4 passion fruit

100ml orange juice

2 tablespoons granulated
sugar

1 teaspoon arrowroot

Cook the ducks as described on page 115. Pour the braising liquor into a jug and allow the fat to rise. Mix 1 tablespoon of fat with the flour. Skim off the remainder, then heat the stock. When boiling, whisk in the flour and fat mixture and cook for a few moments longer. Pour on the wine and stock and stir, then bring to the boil. Simmer for 5 minutes then strain into a clean saucepan.

Scoop out the centres of the passion fruit and mix in a saucepan with the orange juice and sugar. Bring to the boil, then mix 1 teaspoon of the arrowroot with 1 teaspoon of water and stir this in. It acts like a hot jelly in liquid and doesn't have the cloudy, mucous-like quality of cornflour or potato flour. It will lose strength though if cooked too long, so strain the sauce into a jug once you are happy with its consistency.

Plate the legs and carved mallard breasts, then spoon one side with gravy and the other with the passion fruit sauce.

# ROAST PARTRIDGE

Partridge comes in two types: the English Grey or the French Red-legged. Both are reared and shot in Britain so for me there are no issues of patriotism, only quality and price. The Grey are considered superior and are less common, so quite a bit costlier. The Red-legged are small but remarkably good value and you can buy two for less than the price of a sirloin steak.

Small pale-fleshed creatures like these, as in most smaller cuts of meat or fish, will dry out very quickly so need to be stored either with a light brushing of oil or covered by clingfilm as protection. Searing can also dry out the meat, especially delicate types like partridge. I sear most meats but compensate by brushing the surface with olive oil or melted butter, which will soften, whereas air and water will harden and dry – good for salami and salt beef but no good here.

Cut away the legs. This is best achieved by cutting through the skin beneath the breasts so you can see the inside of the legs. Pull the legs away from the carcass until they snap out of the sockets attaching them to the spine. Cut them off with as much meat attached as possible.

Fry the legs, skin-side down until brown, then cover with a 50/50 mixture of red wine and water. Put a lid on the pan and then either simmer slowly over minimal heat or transfer to a moderate oven (150°C/fan 130°C/gas mark 2) for 2 hours.

Thirty minutes before you want to eat, season the crowns with salt and pepper then brown in butter and oil. Roast them at 180°C/fan 160°C/gas mark 4 for 15 minutes. Lift from the oven and leave them to rest for 5 minutes. Carve off the breasts – a sharp knife along each side of the breastbone will do the trick. The insides will still be quite underdone. Brush with cooking liquor and more butter, then return to the oven to finish cooking. This will only take a few more minutes, 5 minutes at most, so you can prepare anything else – vegetables, sauce, reheated legs or whatever at this point. You will have soft breast meat, long-cooked and tender leg meat and the bonus of good cooking liquor to make a sauce or gravy.

# PHEASANT

Pheasant can be treated just like partridge. I will often tap out the breasts between two sheets of clingfilm, lightly so that they become even rather than thin. By doing this you will have uniform cooking rather than a dry tip or underdone wing ends.

HUNTERS PAY MORE FOR THE EXCITEMENT OF SHOOTING...

# Roast partridge with braised lentils and red wine sauce

FOR 6

........................................................................

4 partridge – *braised and roasted as opposite*

25g brown or puy lentils – *drained from the tin, or soaked and cooked weight*

2 rashers of smoked streaky bacon – *cut into dice*

1 shallot – *chopped*

20g butter

1 level tablespoon plain flour

1 tablespoon tomato passata – *or, in an emergency, 1 teaspoon of tomato purée*

50ml red wine

If you use dried lentils – cheaper but you need to be thinking about the meal that much earlier – soak them for 4 hours or overnight, then boil until tender in unsalted water.

Fry the bacon and shallot in the butter, then add the drained lentils and flour.

Cook for a few moments, then stir in the passata and the cooking stock from the braised legs. The stock/cooking liquor from the legs will be full flavoured but probably have too much fat. If you let it rest in a small jug the fat will quickly rise to the surface. Skim it off. Stir in the cooking liquor from the braised legs along with the wine.

Whisk to the boil, and then strain into a jug.

Spoon onto warmed plates, then arrange the breasts and legs of each partridge on top.

# Pheasant pudding with sage and bacon

FOR 6

This is really a warm mousse but with a firmer texture, so calling it pudding meets expectations better. My professional kitchen has access to meat stocks, reduced veal jus, game gravy, etc, but my home kitchen doesn't, so a packet of posh ready-made gravy improved by a shot of amontillado sherry will substitute. The strange brown powders and cubes with their overpowering taste, though, will not help as they are way too salty. If this is all you have, scatter some dressed salad leaves around. You can, if it's easier, use just pheasant breasts (use six), which will produce a whiter but less intensely flavoured pudding.

2 pheasants

4 eggs

500ml double cream

Nutmeg, salt and freshly ground black pepper

Oil – *for frying*

60g dried morel or porcini mushrooms

A little jus or gravy – *if you have it*

6 rashers smoked streaky bacon – *cut into strips*

Sage leaves (*about 3 per serving*)

Bone the pheasants and cut the meat into small dice. Reserve the bones and trimmings.

Process in a food processor until pulped, then add the eggs, one by one, followed by the cream, in a trickle. The mixture will have been warmed by all this, so stir in the seasonings, cover with clingfilm and refrigerate for 1 hour.

Fry the bones and trimmings from the birds in a little oil.

Bring the dried mushrooms to the boil in 50ml water. Strain the mushroom liquor onto the bones and simmer for 30 minutes along with any jus or gravy. Chop the mushrooms.

Strain enough of the liquor over the mushrooms to moisten, then leave to cool.

Preheat the oven to 180°C/fan 160°C/gas mark 4.

Butter six ramekins or dariole moulds, then pipe in the pheasant mixture along the bases and sides so that there is an empty well-like space. Spoon the mushrooms into this and pipe across the remaining mousse.

Place the moulds into a deep ovenproof dish half-filled with warm water then bake until cooked for about 30 minutes.

Turn out the moulds onto warmed soup dishes.

Deep-fry the bacon strips, then the sage leaves and scatter these across.

Pour any remaining liquor or gravy around the puddings.

# Pheasant and chestnut soup with soft spices

A degree of sweetness suits gamey flavours. The unsweetened chestnuts and aromatic rather than fiery spices in this recipe still give a subtle softness to the finished dish.

FOR 6

. . . . . . . . . . . . . . . . . . . . . . . . . . . . . . . . . . . . . . . . . . . . . . .

1 onion - *chopped*

1 carrot – *chopped*

Vegetable oil – *for frying*

1 teaspoon each *ground* cinnamon, cumin, nutmeg and coriander

1 whole pheasant

25g *cooked unsweetened peeled* chestnuts

1.5 litres hot chicken stock

1 tablespoon lemon juice

2 tablespoons double cream

2 tablespoons *chopped* flat-leaf parsley

Salt

Fry the onion and carrot in a little oil in a large heavy-based saucepan or casserole pot, then stir in the spices.

Add the pheasant and let it colour all over.

Add the chestnuts and stock, bring to the boil, cover with a lid and allow to simmer very gently until completely cooked. This will take about 30 minutes.

Carefully lift out the bird, tipping it so that all the liquor in the central cavity returns to the pot rather than scalds your fingers.

When it is just cool enough to handle, cut away all the meat from the bird. Keep a little diced breast meat for the finished soup but return the rest to the pot.

Blend the soup in a liquidiser, and if necessary, strain through a coarse sieve.

Add the lemon juice, cream and a little salt, then stir in the parsley and serve with the smarter-looking pheasant dice you kept aside.

# Roast grouse

FOR 4

Don't fiddle around with birds like grouse or woodcock. A little care in the cooking improves them but all else detracts. They have naturally powerful flavours and are short-term treats best enjoyed simply. Use only young grouse for roasting – older specimens are best braised slowly. For an ideal grouse dinner you will need good gravy, a crouton to sop up any juices from the carved bird and maybe some bread sauce. Game chips – bit like warm crisps – are the traditional potato accompaniment, but small, crisp, roast potatoes are also good. Spreading liver pâté across the crouton features in some recipes for roast grouse, but it doesn't really improve the dish, which has bags of flavour and needs no further help.

4 grouse

50g softened butter

1 tablespoon plain flour

250ml decent red wine

1 teaspoon sugar

4 slices of good white bread, *cut into rounds if liked*

Preheat the oven to 200°C/fan 180°C/gas mark 6.

Rub 30g of the butter over the birds. Roast for 20 minutes, then remove from the oven, baste with the hot butter and juices, and pour off half. Stir the flour into the liquid left in the roasting pan and let this cook for a moment, then stir in the wine and the sugar, to offset the wine's acidity.

Turn the grouse onto their breasts, then return to the oven for 10 minutes. (I prefer grouse to be cooked medium-well, so will add another 5 minutes to my own.) Combine the wine with the cooking juices to make a fine gravy that will only need straining.

Fry the bread in the remaining butter.

Grouse is usually served whole and it's the eater's job to tackle it. If you have any doubts, best to carve off the legs and breasts as this gives an opportunity for a little extra cooking if wanted or needed. Then pile on top of the croutons and serve with watercress, gravy and bread sauce.

## BREAD SAUCE

FOR 4

1 small onion – *peeled*

6 cloves

500ml whole milk

100g fresh breadcrumbs

25g butter

Salt and freshly ground black pepper

A little grated nutmeg

Skewer the onion with the cloves, then place in a saucepan with the milk. Bring to the boil, remove from the heat, then leave to infuse for 15 minutes.

Stir in the breadcrumbs and butter, then cook gently for 10 minutes. Remove the onion, then season with salt, pepper and nutmeg.

HUNTERS PAY MORE FOR THE EXCITEMENT OF SHOOTING...

# Venison pudding

FOR 6

It's easy to add something else to this recipe – cooked salsify or wild mushrooms perhaps. Basically, it is cooked much the same as a steak and kidney pudding and, as with that dish, the suet paste can be rolled into dumplings and steamed on top of the cooking stew instead.

· · · · · · · · · · · · · · · · · · · · · · · · · · · · · · · · · · · · · · · · · · · · · · · · · · · · · · · · · · · · · · · · · · · ·

1 tablespoon olive oil – *plus extra for oiling*

1 large onion – *chopped*

1 carrot – *peeled and chopped*

1 small stick of celery – *peeled and chopped*

700g diced venison

1 tablespoon plain flour

150ml red wine or beer

Salt, freshly ground black pepper and a dash of Worcestershire sauce

### Dough

250g self-raising flour

125g minced suet

Mix the flour, suet and about 75ml of cold water to form a dough.

Oil a 1-litre pudding basin, then roll out the suet dough. Use two-thirds of it to line the base and sides of the basin and keep the rest to cover once the basin has been filled.

Fry the vegetables in the oil, then brown the venison. Stir in the flour, season, then pour in 150ml of cold water along with the wine or beer. Bring to the boil, then turn off the heat and leave to cool.

Fill the pudding basin with this mix and seal with the remaining suet dough. Cover with oiled kitchen foil and wrap the basin in a clean napkin or tea towel. Tie with string and steam for 2 hours.

# Rabbit with mustard crème fraîche and Parma ham

FOR 4

There are two classic preparations of rabbit. One involves prunes which, like the sultana and hare recipe on page 127, contrasts the sweetness of dried fruit with a gamey meat. The other is mustard. Of course, rabbit can also make a decent terrine or a garlic and herb stew. This recipe is a basic braise with mustard, but has the late addition of prosciutto as an extra interest. Morel mushrooms, or indeed truffles if you are feeling rich, would also be rather nice. Rabbit is most often sold cut coarsely into chunks. The back legs are what would be ideal here as the saddle, even in chunks, will tend to be dry by the time the legs are done. But let's be realistic: buy what you can get and make the best of it.

Prosciutto – raw cured ham like those from Parma and San Daniele in Italy, or jamón ibérico from Spain and the Basque country – is a great product. It isn't helped by too much heat, so add it right at the end of the cooking.

25ml vegetable oil

2 rabbits, chopped into large pieces – or 6 legs

15g butter

1 onion – *chopped*

2 garlic cloves – *chopped*

1 tablespoon tomato passata

100ml white wine

600ml hot chicken stock

2 tablespoons Dijon mustard

2 tablespoons crème fraîche

3 tablespoons *chopped* flat-leaf parsley

6 slices of Parma ham – *cut into strips*

Salt and freshly ground black pepper

Heat the oil in a large casserole and brown the rabbit all over.

Lift the meat from the pan and add the butter, then the onion and garlic and cook until soft.

Add the tomato passata, then the wine and stock.

Return the rabbit to the pan and lower the heat to a simmer. Cover with a lid and cook gently for 45 minutes. Lift out the meat.

Stir the mustard and then the crème fraîche into the cooking liquor and simmer for a further few minutes. Season with salt and black pepper.

Stir the parsley into the sauce and pour over the rabbit, then top with the ham.

## FURRED GAME

These aren't quite the bargain of game birds. Hare is quite scarce and deer is popular enough to be expensive. There are both wild and farmed deer to be had. Mostly, the large red deer are farmed, but smaller roe and fallow occasionally appear. Exotic varieties like the small muntjac deer – about the size of a large Labrador – rarely find their way onto the shopping list. The poor old rabbit is just classed as vermin. Wild rabbit has bags of character compared to the farmed version but also, sadly, useless musty offal. You eat the farmed rabbit in spite of the bland meat because the liver and kidney are so good.

> These aren't quite the bargain of game birds

Venison isn't as gelatinous as beef. The bones will flavour a stock but won't be able to give a dense, fuller texture in the way that veal or chicken bones might. If you decide to make a game stock, then add a calf's foot to compensate. The loin from venison can be used much like beef and is best cooked rare or medium rare. I've read that it is a comparatively healthy meat, low in cholesterol and all that, but would remind you that all the oils and butter used to make it a treat, not to mention all the booze-laden sauces, probably counter this happy notion.

## HARE

A hare will have the saddle and the two hind legs that are useable. The forearms need prolonged cooking and will yield little meat, so use them seared along with the bones and cooked for stock.

The saddle or the two fillets from it are best roasted rare. You will need to carefully lift off the membrane that covers the eye of the meat so that it will remain tender after cooking. In traditional dishes in which the whole beast is used, the saddle will be cooked for so long that this rubbery membrane will have melted away. Saddle or rack of lamb has similar problems, as we now eat these joints underdone rather than cooked through.

Jugged hare is the most famous treatment. I'm not entirely sure where the name comes from. One source claims it to be from the meat marinating in a jug before cooking; another, Hannah Glasse, describes the meat being cooked in a jug resting in boiling water while the blood was added. The braise was thickened by adding the hare's blood towards the end of its cooking. This isn't to my taste and evokes childhood memories of the mouthfeel of a visit to the dentist after a couple of extractions. A little blood in liver or in dark meat adds a dimension, black pudding is fine and dandy, but this feels more bravado than pleasure at the dining table. Up to yourself, of course. If you keep the blood, it will need to be mixed with a little vinegar so that it doesn't solidify before cooking.

To prepare hare, use a sharp, pointed knife to cut loose the two fillets that lie either side of the backbone on the saddle. Always cut towards the bone and slide the knife next to but still towards the bone, down and round so that the fillet comes off in one piece. Remove the membrane, then brush the fillets with oil and refrigerate until needed. Cut the bone from each haunch (back leg); you'll see that the meat is formed into definite muscles. Separate these, trim them and cut into dice. This type of treatment is called seam butchery because the dismemberment follows natural lines rather than merely cutting it into equal chunks. The hare dice can be braised and the hare fillets, seared quickly all over, then finished in a moderate oven for 9-10 minutes (160°C/fan 140°C/gas mark 3) until rare.

Carve the fillets into long slices and lay them across the braised hare. How you jazz this up is a matter of taste.

## HARE WITH SULTANAS & BLACK PEPPER

Prepare and cook the hare as described but sprinkle the fillets with coarsely ground black pepper before searing. Heat 2 tablespoons of sultanas in 25ml of Armagnac and 25ml of Madeira or sweet sherry. Leave them to plump up in the booze, then warm through when the hare is nearly done. Add the marinade to the braised hare and sprinkle the sultanas across the top.

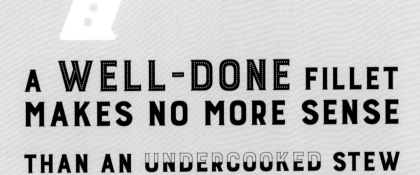

# 7

## A WELL-DONE FILLET MAKES NO MORE SENSE

### THAN AN UNDERCOOKED STEW

Prime cuts like loin or fillet, which need less cooking, have a hefty price tag and will generally be used for grilling, frying or roasting. Forequarter meat – shoulder of lamb, chuck steak and the like – costs less but needs slower cooking to melt away any chewy membranes. Generally, the less work a muscle has had to do, the more tender it will be. Lastly there is the offal, the internal organs, which will give the greatest range of taste and texture, but is really a separate category of ingredient, a slice of lamb's liver having more in common with a slice of calf's liver than either has with a chop or steak. All are good if handled well.

In restaurants we are asked for well-done fillet steak regularly. There is nothing wrong with preferring meat cooked through. In fact, the core flavour of whatever meat it is will be at its most intense this way. But it will be at the cost of texture and the dry, underpowered result of a well-done fillet makes no more sense than an undercooked stew. It's just a waste of money and ingredient when slow-cooked shin or brisket will yield something unctuous and satisfying. My thought is that the diners who want well-done steaks do in fact have taste buds and probably look for the browned outside more than the dry interior.

> Generally, the less work a muscle has had to do the more tender it will be.

Pork has particular baggage, especially amongst those of my own generation, with warnings, many just old wives' tales, over worms and disease if the meat isn't cooked right through. In fact, I am not fond of undercooked white meat of any description. Pink juices running from a veal or pork chop is fine, a good sign that the meat hasn't dried up in fact, but raw stuff in the middle simply doesn't taste good. Iberico, from the black Iberian pig, which is the only pork that has to be served underdone, also happens to be as dark as beef.

In another capacity, I have studied food taboos. There are plenty, but pork is the one that always springs to mind. A credit to the tenacity of Jews and Muslims everywhere. A restricted diet is a common feature of dining rituals of ancient civilisations, as it gives people a sense of common purpose and of exclusivity. Pork will always be a prime candidate for taboo. For a start, of all the animals we eat, pig flesh closely resembles that of humans. That's why pigs' organs are successfully transplanted into humans, so all a bit creepy. Mostly, though, eating pork appears to be a Semitic problem. In ancient Egypt pre-sewage systems, pigs were used as the communal waste disposal because they are content to eat excrement – bit like my Labrador. It was evidently fine to own and to eat pork at that point, but the poor old swineherds were considered unclean and barred from the temples. The god of evil, Seth, developed a pig's head in contrast to decent deities like Horus, who had a falcon head, or the protective goddess Hathor, who had a cow by way of topping. Things deteriorated over the millennia for the consumption of pork in the ancient Near East, and today religious belief forbids Muslims throughout the world to eat pork in any form.

# GRILLING AND ROASTING

Buying good-quality meat is essential if it is to be exposed to intense direct heat because there is little in the way of safety net for your chops or roast beef if the result is cheaper but dry or tasteless. That said, it is easy to bugger good meat up through careless handling and cooking. First, the handling: keep the meat either covered with clingfilm or brushed with oil until it is due to be cooked and eaten. The enemy is always dryness. Lamb is undoubtedly the best bet if you have any doubts. It's free range for a start, though the texture develops quickly as the animal develops from a quasi-veal, milk-fed, meat – not my taste – to a one-year-old when it's called hogget – lots of flavour but starting to border on mutton. Mutton is nasty, same as goat, and stinks of toilets and old age. The practice of spreading vinegar and mint alongside redcurrant jam all over mutton chops has its roots in disguising this – never understood why anyone would do this to a tender delicate rack of lamb.

Pork is a separate story. Until the 1990s it rarely appeared on restaurant menus except as ham or bacon and it became a largely domestic ingredient. I started to believe that everything I knew about cooking pork was mistaken until I realised that it was the pork itself that had changed. Animals that have been bred to be lean are okay for braised shoulder or roast belly, but poor and inadequate for chops and roast loin. Buy rare breeds – Gloucester Old Spot, Middle Whites, Tamworth or Berkshire – that have natural fat and are generally reared by enthusiasts not as prone to cut costs on feed quality and living conditions. Supermarkets are useless for the producers of this sort of pork. Instead, buy from small operations, ones that are investing in a traditional product that is below the radar for the behemoth of supermarket purchasing.

You need high heat to sear anything grilled, fried or even small joints like racks for roasting, but only for a short time or the meat will dry out. Brush your meat with olive oil, then sear quickly in a preheated dry frying pan. Alternatively, heat butter and oil in the pan and use this to brown the outsides of the meat. Lift the meat onto a warm roasting tin and then finish the cooking at lower temperature. All chops, steaks and roasts need resting for a while once done. This doesn't imply a little lie-down or catch-up on sleep. It's to allow the heat from the outer part of whatever has been cooked to slowly penetrate the centre, giving a more even cooking level to whatever steak or joint is being cooked. Resting also lets a red hue develop at the centre of a piece of lamb or beef while the actual flesh transforms from raw to lightly done. A steak will need just 2 or 3 minutes resting, but a rib of beef or leg of pork will take much longer, at least 15 minutes, possibly half an hour. This provides an ideal opportunity to make gravy, cook side vegetables, heat plates, have a large gin and tonic, whatever you need most, and don't forget that it will be only the outside meat that cools, so a swift revisit to the oven or pan will return everything to hot and ready to eat in moments.

> The enemy is always dryness.

# Wiener schnitzel

FOR 4

Think white meat, batted flat or at least flattish, then breadcrumbed and fried. A true Wiener schnitzel is made with veal, but in truth pork is just as good and so is chicken. There is a common theme to this sort of dish. Italians call the treatment 'Milanese' when it's with veal, but really the idea is the same as for southern fried chicken (see page 102) or even fish fingers. The crumb coating will protect the meat like a savoury skin while keeping the centre soft and succulent.

There are a few basics. Don't flatten the meat too thinly or it will taste of fried breadcrumbs and little else. I like the meat to be upwards of 1cm thick. Fried stuff needs the contrast of something acidic, so either lemon juice or a sharp salad as an accompaniment. There are variants on the dish. The most popular is called veal Holstein, which involves little more than the addition of a fried egg, some capers and anchovy to the top. In the French kitchen, both Wiener schnitzel, which is called escalope de veau viennoise, and Holstein get drenched with heated butter before serving. This is a poor idea – a crisp schnitzel with a tender meat centre is not improved by making its crust soggy and greasy. Escalope in French and Schnitzel in German just mean something sliced. I'm calling the slices of meat escalope and the breadcrumbed result, schnitzel.

4 x 100g veal escalopes

3 eggs, *beaten*

100g white breadcrumbs – panko is fine

Lard for frying – or vegetable oil plus a knob of butter

Salt and freshly ground black pepper

Tap out the escalopes to 1cm thick. The flattening is partly to tenderise the meat and is easily accomplished by putting the escalopes between two sheets of clingfilm then, if you have no cutlet bat, using the flat side of a heavy knife or the base of a small saucepan to produce an even result.

Season the escalopes with salt and black pepper, then egg and breadcrumb each.

Spoon enough lard or oil and butter into a frying pan to give 0.5cm depth and heat this. You need the fat to be hot enough to seal and crisp the schnitzels without burning them and you can test for this by dropping a piece of bread into the pan – it should sizzle and then turn golden.

Fry the escalopes, one at a time unless you have an enormous pan. You may need to strain the fat, wipe the pan free of burning crumbs, then return the lard or oil so that each subsequent schnitzel is as good as the first.

# Pork in shirtsleeves

FOR 4

Beef Wellington is classic treatment of beef fillet, seared and wrapped in puff pastry before being baked. It's a method that works well with boned grouse or wood pigeon, and also with pork fillet, trimmed of all the white membrane. There will be no gravy produced so either a crisp salad or a soft vegetable purée will be called for alongside.

Scraps of puff pastry are actually better than a pristine just-made confection for this dish. You want the crispness and crunch of a butter puff pastry but not the rising. You can make this in individual portions or as whole wrapped fillets (one fillet will normally make two generous portions). In either case it will look better cut into four if a whole fillet, or into two if individual ones. No point taking all this effort and then presenting what appears to be a large sausage roll.

2 pork fillets

2 tablespoons wholegrain mustard

600g butter puff pastry

1 egg, *beaten*, for eggwash

**For the stuffing**

2 tablespoons olive oil

1 small onion, *finely chopped*

2 garlic cloves, *crushed*

3 rashers of unsmoked streaky bacon, *chopped*

150g button mushrooms, *finely chopped*

1 tablespoon double cream

Salt and freshly ground black pepper

**For the pancake batter**

2 eggs

Vegetable oil

250ml whole milk

100g plain flour

First make the stuffing. Heat half the oil and fry the onion, garlic and bacon, then add the mushrooms. As they cook they will produce liquid. Mix in the cream, season with a little salt and black pepper, then gently cook until dry.

Next make the pancakes. Whisk together the eggs, 1 tablespoon oil, a little of the milk and the flour until smooth, then whisk in the remaining milk and a pinch of salt until you have a batter the consistency of single cream. Heat a frying pan and wipe it completely clean. Brush with oil, then pour in a couple of tablespoons of batter. Tilt the pan so the batter coats the base evenly. When set flip the pancake briefly. Continue until you have enough pancakes to wrap around both fillets.

Season the pork, then sear in a hot pan. Reduce the heat and allow to cook gently for a few minutes on each side. The meat should be nearly, but not entirely, cooked through.

Brush the meat with the wholegrain mustard. Press the stuffing onto the pancakes and lay the seared fillets across the middle. Wrap the pancakes and stuffing around the meat.

Roll out the pastry to a thickness of 3mm, then cover the fillets. Seal the edges by pinching the pastry and if necessary brushing with water. Turn each pastry parcel over and brush with beaten egg. Refrigerate for 30 minutes, then brush with egg once more.

Preheat the oven to 180°C/fan 160°C/gas mark 4. Place the fillets on a baking sheet, then score curved lines lightly with a knife tip into the pastry. Bake for 20 minutes.

A WELL-DONE FILLET MAKES NO MORE SENSE THAN AN UNDERCOOKED STEW

# Rump of lamb with potato and olive cakes

You will need a rump per person. These joints represent very good value and are one of my favourites. Once cooked, rest the meat for at least 5 minutes before carving. Also, remember to carve them across rather than along the grain of the meat to keep the meat tender.

FOR 4

4 rumps of lamb

6 anchovy fillets – brown ones from a jar or tin

4 garlic cloves – *crushed*

Olive oil – *for brushing*

A few rosemary leaves

175ml white wine

1 teaspoon Dijon mustard

Salt and freshly ground black pepper

**Potato and olive cakes**

500g maincrop potatoes – *peeled then cut into equal-sized pieces*

50g tinned green olives stuffed with anchovy – one third of an average tin

1 tablespoon *chopped* flat-leaf parsley

1 egg yolk, plus 1 large egg – *beaten*, for eggwash

100g fresh breadcrumbs

Olive oil

Stab six slits into each rump using a sharp pointed knife.

Quarter the anchovy fillets, then poke one piece plus a little crushed garlic into each slit. Grind some black pepper over each rump and brush with a little olive oil. Leave to marinate for at least 1 hour but ideally overnight.

Boil the potatoes in salted water, then drain, mash and leave to cool. Try not to overcook the potatoes or they will be very soft to handle. Chop the olives and mix these into the potato along with the parsley and egg yolk. Form into golf ball-shaped patties and pass each through eggwash and breadcrumbs. Shape these into cakes and refrigerate until needed.

Preheat the oven to 180°C/fan 160°C/gas mark 4.

Sear each rump in a hot pan until each starts to colour. Add the rosemary to the pan then transfer everything to a roasting tin. Pour over the white wine, season the lamb with salt, then roast for 15 minutes until medium rare.

While the lamb rests, fry the potato and olive cakes in 0.5cm of oil until crisp on each side.

Pour the cooking juices from the lamb and the mustard into a liquidiser and blend.

Carve each rump into three slices and serve with the potato cakes and a spoonful of the blended cooking juices.

# Lamb shoulder shanks with butter beans and chorizo

Meat from the lamb shoulder is way better than that of leg. Maybe the awkward carving and occasional lumps of fat have put people off this as a roasting joint. With shanks this is no problem. A shoulder shank is the same as a leg shank, only slightly smaller, cheaper and nicer.

Let the meat cook slow and long, for a couple of hours, so that the meat falls off the bone and all the flavours mix together to make a satisfying dish. The dish is simple to make but does demand the patience or foresight to begin cooking a couple of hours before you want to eat. No other fancy footwork required.

FOR 4

2 tablespoons olive oil

4 shoulder shanks

1 onion – *chopped*

2 large garlic cloves – *chopped*

400g tin chopped tomatoes

400g tin butter beans – *drained*

50g cooking chorizo – *cubed or sliced*

1 glass white wine

Flat-leaf parsley – *finely chopped*

Salt and freshly ground black pepper

Warm the oil in a heavy-based pan or ovenproof casserole, then brown the shanks on all sides and season with salt and black pepper. Add the onion and garlic, then the tomatoes, butter beans and chorizo. Let this bubble for 5 minutes, then add the wine and the same amount of cold water. Place a lid on the pot, then turn down the heat to a slow simmer, or transfer to a moderate to low oven (150°C/fan 130°C/gas mark 2), for 2 hours. Check every 30 minutes and add a little more liquid if needed. Serve with plenty of chopped parsley.

A WELL-DONE FILLET MAKES NO MORE SENSE THAN AN UNDERCOOKED STEW

# Blade of beef with red wine

FOR 4

The steaks from the blade bone area of beef are often called feather steaks because they have a feather-like membrane running though the centre. In the US, this cut is called a flatiron steak and is generally served rare. I prefer it braised so that instead of being some poor man's version of a rump steak with a membrane across the middle, it becomes a deeply flavoured braised steak. The retention of its shape and size will reassure your diners that it is a steak they are eating. Cubed or diced meat tends to imply something more downmarket. No bother to me, but in presentation terms, a larger cut of meat, even braised meat, has more presence than a bowl of small chunks. This recipe calls for a lot of red wine, so probably costs more than a grilled steak whichever way you served it.

The seasoning here is merely a touch of star anise. Don't use too much. You can add whatever your favourite flavouring might be, but the powerful beef and red wine tastes will be predominant, and really this is the objective anyway.

4 x 200g feather steaks

A little vegetable oil
– *for frying*

100g each *diced* carrot, celery and onion

4 garlic cloves

500ml cheap, but not nasty, red wine

½ star anise

100g lardons

100g chestnut mushrooms – *cut into quarters*

Salt and freshly ground black pepper

Preheat the oven to 170°C/fan 150°C/gas mark 4.

Season the steaks with salt and black pepper then fry them in a little oil until well coloured and place in a heavy-based casserole or deep roasting tin. Fry the vegetables and garlic, then add these to the casserole. Top up with the wine and 500ml of cold water – the liquid should cover the meat – then add the star anise.

Cover and bring to the boil. Transfer to the oven and simmer gently for 1½ hours.

Strain the cooking juices into a separate saucepan and reduce while the rest of the dish is finished.

Fry the lardons, then the mushrooms and spoon over the steaks and coat with the reduced cooking juices. Serve with potato, either mashed or new, depending on the season.

# Calf's sweetbreads with sauerkraut

FOR 4

Sweetbreads are one of those words that provoke macho approval. In fact, sweetbread is a portmanteau word covering all white offal, usually from calves or lambs. Not just testicles. The two glands most used are in fact the thymus, sometimes called throat breads, and the pancreas, which is generally sold as heart breads because of their fist shape. Neither has any connection with the trouser area, but they are expensive. Heart breads are easily the finer and have featured on my every menu as a treat for those who like this sort of stuff, but you rarely see it on sale or on restaurant menus.

A small portion will make an exquisite starter to a fish main course in a grand meal, but the dish itself, with a little salad, maybe a few Jersey Royal potatoes if they are in season and a glass or two of decent red Burgundy, will be enough of a treat for anyone.

I use German sauerkraut from a jar. It will have been fermented then washed and mixed with white wine, so not too fierce or too salty. Much more pleasant than all that Korean kimchi which is about the place now or the tongue-numbing ferments from Russia and Poland.

Points to watch:

The preparation of this dish has two distinct parts. The sweetbreads have to be soaked for 1 hour in cold water, then blanched – brought to the boil in an aromatic stock – and allowed to cool in this cooking liquor so that they are firm and set, but still soft. This is best done 1 hour or so before you want to complete and serve the dish.

Use your head when choosing a pan to blanch the sweetbreads. A vast one that holds gallons of water will take forever to boil and probably reduce below the level of the sweetbreads while doing so, thus cooking them unevenly or too much. A saucepan that takes the meat plus 1 litre of water will be ideal, and a circle of greaseproof paper across the top as it comes to the boil will also be an advantage, holding in the heat and allowing the liquid to come to a gentle simmer while you can keep an eye on what's happening.

The sauce is a warm dressing thickened with a mustardy mayonnaise. It will separate if boiled hard for too long, so try not to.

750g calf's sweetbreads

1 shallot – *chopped*

1 teaspoon white
wine vinegar

A little olive oil

25g butter

4 generous tablespoons
sauerkraut

Squeeze of lemon

Salt and freshly ground
black pepper

**For the dressing**

1 egg yolk

1 tablespoon white
wine vinegar

1 level tablespoon
Dijon mustard

1 tablespoon white
wine vinegar

3 tablespoons olive oil

Dash of Tabasco sauce

Salt and freshly ground
black pepper

1 tablespoon *chopped*
flat-leaf parsley

Preheat the oven to 180°C/fan 160°C/gas mark 4.

Trim the sweetbreads. They often come with bits of tube attached, which all look rather medical. Cut these away, also most but not all of the white outer skin – a little is needed to hold the sweetbreads in one piece. Soak the sweetbreads in cold water for 1 hour to remove any specks of blood.

Place in a saucepan and add the shallot, vinegar and just enough cold water to cover. Put a circle of greaseproof paper on top and bring to the boil. Simmer for a few minutes only. You are looking for a soft yet firm feel. Turn off the heat and leave until needed. If this isn't for a day or two, then transfer the meat and cooking liquor to a container and refrigerate until wanted.

Make the dressing just like a weak mayonnaise. Stir the egg yolk, vinegar and mustard together, then slowly whisk in the and seasonings.

Lift the sweetbreads from the liquid and pat dry. If the sizes are too unequal, then slice the larger sweetbreads into two or even three. Season with salt and black pepper, then brush with olive oil.

Heat a dry ovenproof pan and, when very hot, sear the sweetbreads until golden. You may need to do this in batches as they are prone to leak a lot of liquid.

Add the butter and finish cooking in the oven (or under a grill) while you finish the dish. They will have been cooked by the blanching, but need to be golden brown on the outside and hot in the centre.

Heat the sauerkraut in a little cooking liquor, then spoon onto warmed plates.

Whisk the dressing into a couple of tablespoons of cooking liquor, then spoon this onto the plates also.

Place the sweetbreads next to these and dress with a final squeeze of lemon and a drizzle of olive oil.

# Maksalaatikko Finnish liver pudding with lingonberries

FOR 4

This recipe reads as a little odd but the flavours work together perfectly in a rustic and hearty way. It's best hot but when cold forms a central part of Finland's version of smorgasbord – *voileipapoyta*. Rice may not be the local crop in Scandinavia, but it has been part of celebratory eating for ages and a rice pudding will round off the traditional Christmas dinner. Use pig or ox liver for preference. Lamb's liver is okay but alters the flavour, and calves or chicken liver is just too delicate.

Lingonberries are related to cranberries but have a distinctive taste. They are very acidic so will need a little sugar. I buy them frozen in 1kg packs from the Scandinavian Kitchen in London, but they are available elsewhere and online. Lingonberry jam isn't difficult to find but is too sweet for my taste. I prefer the berries to have retained a good deal of their sharpness to cut through the liver and rice pudding. Redcurrants or cranberries will perform the same task of course, but not as well.

1 teaspoon salt

150g short-grain rice

1 litre whole milk

25g butter

1 onion, *finely chopped*

400g pig's liver

2 eggs

60ml treacle

100g raisins

½ teaspoon dried marjoram

Salt and freshly ground white pepper

**To garnish**

4 tablespoons lingonberries

1 tablespoon granulated sugar

Bring 200ml of cold water and the salt to the boil. Add the rice then, stirring continuously to prevent sticking, boil until the water evaporates.

Add the milk, reduce the heat, cover and simmer for about 30 minutes, or until the rice is cooked through.

Preheat the oven to 180°C/fan 160°C/gas mark 4. Grease an ovenproof dish with a little of the butter, then melt the remainder in a saucepan, add the onion and cook gently for 5 minutes until soft but not browned. Stir in the cooked rice and season with salt and pepper.

Cut the liver into small chunks, then chop in the food processor until fine but not puréed. You can chop by hand if uncertain. Transfer to a bowl. Add the eggs, treacle, raisins, marjoram and white pepper and mix thoroughly. Combine with the cooked rice.

Spoon the mixture into the buttered ovenproof dish and bake for 1¼ hours, or until the pudding feels firm when pressed with an upturned fork or spoon.

For the garnish, heat the lingonberries and sugar. Bring to the boil. Serve wedges of pudding with berries on the side or separately.

A WELL-DONE FILLET MAKES NO MORE SENSE THAN AN UNDERCOOKED STEW

# Beef tartare

FOR 4

Ideally the meat for a tartare should be chopped rather than minced or processed. Steak tartare is rather like bloody Mary in that spice level is a matter of personal taste. I love spicy food but oddly I don't like overly spicy steak tartare as it tends to overpower the meat flavour. The ratio of Worcestershire sauce and Tabasco to meat will be critical. Too much makes it difficult to eat; too little and it will taste like meat you have forgotten to cook. Be guided by your own taste buds and if you are entertaining others, then err on the side of caution and offer the bottle of Worcestershire sauce and Tabasco separately.

The health police who worry on your behalf about restaurants stipulate that we in the catering trade do a little more than required at home. Most bacteria are on the surface of a cut piece of meat so we have to sear the outside of the fillet before thinly slicing off and disposing of the scorched surface to leave pristine meat not previously exposed to the air. You can do this as well if you wish. Venison works equally well, though it will usually be the eye of the meat from its loin rather than the comparatively tiny fillets that fit the bill.

The traditional accompaniments are hot, crisp chips and a salad. There are no better.

8 anchovies

2 egg yolks

1 tablespoon Dijon mustard

1 tablespoon white wine vinegar

1 tablespoon olive oil

500g trimmed beef fillet

4 medium-sized gherkins

1 tablespoon capers

1 shallot

2 tablespoons flat-leaf parsley

2 hard-boiled eggs

Worcestershire sauce

Tabasco sauce

Salt and freshly ground black pepper

Crush the anchovies, then stir in the egg yolks, mustard, vinegar and olive oil.

Chop the beef fillet, then finely chop the gherkins, capers, shallot and parsley, and push the hard-boiled eggs through a sieve. Combine with the anchovy mixture. Add the Tabasco and Worcestershire sauces until the spice level suits. Don't forget to serve with hot, thin chips.

# Lamb's sweetbreads pies

FOR 4

Lambs' sweetbreads are smaller than calves' but much easier to source and also much cheaper. Butchers will have this sort of thing in stock but supermarkets, anxious to sell you what is easiest for themselves, may need a day or two's notice. I use a smaller version of these pies in my restaurant alongside some roasted rack of lamb to make a dish contrasting the textures of these different parts of the same beast. You can, of course, do the same if you want.

24 lambs' sweetbreads

10ml white wine

8 fresh or soaked dried morel mushrooms

10ml olive oil

2 shallots – *chopped*

1 large chicken breast or 2 small ones

2 eggs

A grinding of nutmeg

50ml double cream

1kg puff pastry

Salt and freshly ground black pepper

Preheat the oven to 180°C/fan 160°C/gas mark 4.

Poach the sweetbreads for 3–4 minutes in just enough water and the wine to cover. They should be set but not hard. Leave to cool in the cooking liquor.

Pat the sweetbreads dry, then cut into medium-sized dice. Lambs' sweetbreads aren't very large, so this will probably involve just quartering them. Cut the morels into similar-sized pieces, then fry them with the sweetbreads and shallots, brushing the sweetbreads with oil beforehand, until they start to colour. Season with salt and black pepper and put to one side.

Dice then blend the chicken breast in a food processor. Add the eggs, nutmeg, seasonings and cream, then blend for a few more moments.

Roll out the puff pastry as thinly as you can, then cut into eight rounds, about 16cm in diameter – you want two per portion.

Stir the sweetbread mix into the chicken mousse. Spoon the mixture into the centre of four pastry rounds. Moisten the edges with cold water and cover each with a second pastry round. Refrigerate until needed.

Bake the pies for about 30 minutes.

A WELL-DONE FILLET MAKES NO MORE SENSE THAN AN UNDERCOOKED STEW

# BUDAPEST IS A PARADISE FOR THE GREEDY

The word pudding has hefty connotations not properly understood by those who call the sweet course dessert, but 'pudding' can mean some confection as light as a sorbet, not just suet and sponge jobs for a winter's day. And cake, though quite possibly rounding off the meal, usually signifies something that needs a cup of tea or coffee, at most a glass of Madeira, by way of accompaniment.

Some of the most successful versions of cake as dessert involve very plain creations, superficially at least. Albergo del Sole, an inn south of Milan, offered one of the finest sabbiosa con crema di mascarpone, a plain pound cake served warm with a ladleful of mascarpone sabayon. Flourless chocolate cakes make serviceable puds as well. The soft, fondant centres have almost reached cliché status on restaurant menus but they are light enough to manage, maybe with a few poached cherries or apricots and a dollop of crème fraîche, even after a substantial meal.

> When visiting my in-laws in Finland, a coffee table that would pass for a three-course meal would appear sporting grand gâteau-style jobs, biscuits and sweet bread.

Germans and Scandinavians like a slice of cake too. When visiting my in-laws in Finland, a coffee table that would pass for a three-course meal would appear sporting grand gâteau-style jobs, biscuits and sweet bread. It was the coffee equivalent of afternoon tea at the Ritz or Fortnum & Mason but, in the nicest possible way, less genteel. No raised pinky, just a hearty appetite called for.

For me though, Vienna and Budapest are tops. Forget about boys' choirs and goulash, there are acres of strudel, cherry and curd cheese not just apple, Esterhazy cake, Sachertorte, plum and poppy seed dumplings, the sort of stuff that no slimming regime will ever include. My first encounters with Austro-Hungarian food came in 1970 when I worked in the kitchens of the Gay Hussar restaurant in Soho, initially making hefty stews and dumplings before moving on to making cakes and puds. One such, Somloi, a trifle flavoured with crushed walnuts, apricot and rum then drizzled with melted chocolate and a spoonful of whipped cream, has featured on my dessert menus ever since.

Vienna's coffee houses sport celebrated cakes. Demel, a gloriously kitsch and long-established coffee house on the Kohlmarkt, claims to make the best version of the Hotel Sacher's eponymous chocolate cake and there are always a dozen or so Konditorei (pastry shops) jostling for top status. I spent an afternoon at the Sacher attempting to match their cake with dessert wine. None of them worked so I opted for one of Willi Opitz's stunning sweet wines on the assumption that they could at least be consumed separately and with equal pleasure. Watch out for the words 'mit Schlag' which signify serious amounts of whipped cream on top of whatever is in place already.

Budapest is much the same paradise for the greedy and my experience is that the gypsy violins that partner most meals are even better here. The Café Gerbeaud in Vörösmarty Square, on the Pest side of the Danube, has been serving traditional pastries to go with first-rate coffee since 1850 and is worth the ticket to Budapest all by itself.

# Madeira cake

### FOR 6–8

Perfect with a pot of tea or cup of coffee, not just a glass of sweet wine. The standard test for doneness is a skewer or sharp knife inserted into the centre of the cake. If the skewer comes out clean, the cake it is ready. Madeira cake keeps well, in fact it tastes better the day after baking.

170g unsalted butter
– *at room temperature,*
*plus extra for greasing*

170g caster sugar

Grated zest of 1 orange and
1 lemon, plus 1 tablespoon
lemon juice

4 eggs

170g plain flour

Scant teaspoon
baking powder

Pinch salt

Preheat the oven to 170°C/fan 150°C/gas mark 3. Grease a 225g loaf tin with butter.

Cream the butter, sugar and zests together – a food processor or electric beater will be fine – then beat in the eggs, one at a time. Next, add the lemon juice, flour, baking powder and salt.

Spoon the batter into the prepared loaf tin and bake for 1 hour. Leave to cool for a while before turning out onto a wire rack.

# Orange and almond cake

This cake will serve as a pudding. It is softened with syrup and Grand Marnier in much the same way as rum baba but contains no flour so will suit those on a gluten-free regime.

FOR 6–10

2 oranges

6 eggs

250g caster sugar

1 tablespoon baking powder

250g ground almonds

**To finish**

50g granulated sugar

2 tablespoons Grand Marnier

Boil the oranges in water for about 3 hours until very soft. Cool then halve to scrape out the pips and juice. Blend in a food processor, then drain away as much liquid as possible. You will need around 300g chopped orange pulp and skin in total.

Preheat the oven to 150°C/fan 130°C/gas mark 2. Line a 20cm round tin with sides 6cm deep with baking parchment.

Whisk the eggs, sugar, baking powder and almonds together – for 1 minute if you are using an electric whisk, or for a couple of minutes otherwise – then add the orange. Whisk for the same amount of time again.

Pour the batter into the prepared tin and bake on the middle shelf of the oven for 1 hour. Meanwhile, put the granulated sugar and 50ml cold water in a small saucepan and bring to the boil. Once the sugar has dissolved remove from the heat and leave to cool.

Remove the cake from the oven and allow to cool to the touch before spiking the top surface of the cake all over with a skewer. Soak with the sugar syrup mixed with the Grand Marnier.

# Chocolate cake

There's very little flour involved, so this cake may be left a little underdone with no ill effect. What flour there is, isn't wheat flour, so it is also gluten-free.

FOR 6–10

225g plain chocolate or couverture – *grated*

100g unsalted butter

4 eggs – *separated*

225g icing sugar

A few drops of vanilla extract

2 tablespoons cornflour

Preheat the oven to 190°C/fan 170°C/gas mark 5. Line an 18cm round cake tin with baking parchment.

Melt the chocolate and butter together by putting both in a bowl standing in warm water. Stir now and again.

Whisk the egg whites until stiff.

Whisk the egg yolks, icing sugar and vanilla together until the mixture lightens perceptibly. Stir in the cornflour.

Whisk the melted chocolate and butter into the yolks and sugar mixture, then fold in the whisked egg white one-third at a time.

Spoon the batter into the tin and bake for 30–40 minutes.

## CHOCOLATE

Chocolate, a confection of vanilla, sugar and cocoa solids, can vary dramatically in both quality and sweetness. A general rule is that the higher the cocoa content the better the chocolate. But things aren't quite that simple. Very high concentrations of cocoa make for bitter chocolate. The more cocoa in relation to sugar, the more bitter the chocolate that results, and most importantly, the quality of fat added if it should be anything other than cocoa butter, is crucial to the final greasiness or otherwise of the finished product.

Couverture is a style of chocolate used by chocolatiers. It contains a high level of cocoa solids – anything from 50% to 90%, depending on what's wanted for the recipe – and is the building block for most chocolate pralines or truffles. It's not a product designed to be eaten as it is, but rather to be melted. It's then either mixed with booze or cream to make ganache for truffles, or tempered to produce a glossy, stable finish for dipping liqueurs and pralines, or for making Easter eggs.

Without wishing to overcomplicate things, chocolate is composed of two types of crystal. One produces a glossy and crisp finish, the other flabby and dull. If couverture is melted to a specific temperature then cooled – melt to 40°C, cool to 27°C, then warm gently to 31°C – then it is possible to seed the second, flabby crystal so that all are the same. The chocolate that has been through this process is called 'tempered' and the point of this procedure is to produce a crisper, shinier result. Once cooled and set, tempered chocolate will shrink slightly and this aspect is essential in chocolate making for it means that Easter eggs and pralines can be snapped easily from their moulds while still setting to a firm finish.

# Túrós palacsinta

FOR 4–6

Not sure that pancakes qualify as cake, though these Hungarian cheese pancakes are good as a dessert or with coffee. They are also very easy to make and there can be times when this is an endearing characteristic. The super-lazy could even buy pancakes rather than make them because most supermarkets sell quite decent-quality specimens. The cheese is more important. Some places such as delicatessens sell cream cheese – and curd cheese, which is similar – by weight. If you cannot source this sort of cheese, be wary of what you buy as substitute. Mascarpone is okay but most cream cheese spreads sold in tubs are heavily salted, designed to partner smoked salmon not sugar and orange peel.

### Batter

100g plain flour

200ml skimmed milk

1 teaspoon caster sugar

2 eggs

1 teaspoon vegetable oil

### Filling

250g cream cheese or curd cheese

1 egg yolk

50g caster sugar

Grated zest and juice of ½ orange

Grated zest and juice of ½ lemon

2 drops of vanilla extract

2 tablespoons sultanas

Icing sugar – *for dusting*

Whisk the pancake batter ingredients together. Apparently, pancake batter improves with age – not something I have noticed particularly – so you could make this a little in advance if it suits. Heat a (preferably) non-stick 20cm pan, then pour in enough batter to form a thin pancake. Toss or flip the pancake briefly, then make another, and another, until the batter is finished.

Mix together the filling ingredients and spoon into the centre of each pancake. Roll into a cigar shape and then heat briefly in the oven or microwave. Dust with icing sugar and serve.

# Bakewell tart

FOR 6–10

Bakewell tart is known as Bakewell pudding in the eponymous Derbyshire town. The essential flavour combination of ground almonds, sugar, butter and eggs is called frangipane and the same tart will work well without the jam and with, say, some poached pears or apricots instead. Similarly, ground walnuts or hazelnuts in place of almonds with a decorative sprinkling of halved roasted specimens on top will make an equally tasty tart.

## Sweet pastry

75g caster sugar

75g ground almonds

225g plain flour – *plus extra for dusting*

175g unsalted butter

2 egg yolks

## Frangipane

250g unsalted butter – *at room temperature*

250g caster sugar

4 eggs – *beaten*

250g ground almonds

Raspberry jam

Make the pastry by processing together the dry ingredients then adding the butter and egg yolk. Rest the dough for an hour then roll out on floured clingfilm to a thickness of 3mm. Lift and turn the pastry onto a deep-sided 25cm tart case, then pull away the clingfilm. The pastry will be awkward to handle. Don't worry. Trim the sides and press patches of pastry into whatever parts are bare – just like plasticine. Let the tart case rest in the fridge for an hour.

Preheat the oven to 180°C/fan 160°C/gas mark 4, remove the tart case from the fridge and bake blind (without filling) for 20 minutes.

Meanwhile, prepare the frangipane. Cream together the butter and sugar, beat in the eggs, one at a time, then fold in the ground almonds.

Remove the tart case from the oven. Push down any bumps that have risen in the base, spread first with a layer of raspberry jam, then with the almond mixture. Bake for 30 minutes.

# Iced nougat parfait

This needs a compote or purée of fruit to make the dish complete. The choice is yours but I have used plums, rhubarb and mango in this role.

FOR 6

100g flaked almonds

70g icing sugar

300ml double cream

50ml Cointreau

100g clear honey

Juice of ½ lemon

Zest of 1 orange – *grated*

50g caster sugar

5 egg whites

Coat the almonds in the icing sugar then toast – or bake – until brown. This is best achieved on a baking sheet under a grill or at the top of a hot – 220°C/fan 200°C/gas mark 7 – oven. Watch the almonds throughout as they burn soon after they are perfect. Cool then crush the almonds – not too finely.

Whip the cream, adding the booze as it thickens. Line a small loaf tin, terrine or deep dish with clingfilm, allowing it to hang over the sides.

Bring the honey, lemon juice, orange zest and sugar and to the boil in a large pan.

Whisk the egg whites until stiff, then trickle on the hot honey and lemon mix off the heat. Keep whisking until the parfait mix is cold.

Fold in the whipped cream, then spoon the parfait into the prepared tin and freeze.

Remove from the freezer 20 minutes before you want to serve. Turn out using the clingfilm and cut into slices.

# Somloi

FOR 8

This version of trifle is perennially popular in central Europe. I have seen cherries substituted for apricot and also, in Vienna inevitably, mountains of whipped cream used. This recipe is my favourite and has appeared on my menus in winter for years.

The general idea is two layers of sponge, brushed with crushed walnuts, apricot compote and rum, sandwiching plenty of pastry cream, which needs to be on the solid side. The result is cut into squares then covered with some lightly whipped cream and drizzled with melted chocolate. Lots of calories.

· · · · · · · · · · · · · · · · · · · · · · · · · · · · · · · · · · · · · · · · · · · · · · · · · · · ·

**Sponge**

4 medium eggs

100g caster sugar

100g plain flour

**Pastry cream**

200g caster sugar

6 egg yolks

750ml milk

2 vanilla pods – *split and the seeds scraped into the milk*

100g plain flour

**Paste**

75g walnuts

75g apricot compote – tinned or jarred

75g apricot jam

6 tablespoons dark rum

**To finish**

300ml double cream – *lightly whipped*

50g dark chocolate *melted* with a knob of butter

Preheat the oven to 190°C/fan 170°C/gas mark 5.

For the sponge, whisk the eggs and sugar to ribbon stage – when the mixture is thick enough to form ribbons when you lift the whisk. Fold in the flour. Spoon the batter into a non-stick, 5cm deep, 23cm square baking tin, then bake for 20 minutes. Turn out onto a wire rack and allow to cool.

Make the pastry cream. Whisk half the sugar with the egg yolks until thick and creamy. Put the remaining sugar in a pan with the milk and vanilla and bring to the boil. Whisk the flour into the egg yolk and sugar mix, then slacken the result with a ladleful of boiling milk. Stir this until thick, then whisk into the hot milk. Stir to the boil – it will thicken quite a bit – then sieve into a bowl and leave to cool. Sprinkle a little sugar over the cooling pastry cream so that no skin forms.

Grind the walnuts, apricot compote, jam and rum into a grainy paste.

Assemble the trifle. Slice the sponge horizontally into two. Lay one piece – cut-side uppermost – onto a deep dish. Spread half the walnut paste over the sponge. Spoon on the cooled pastry cream, then spread remaining paste over the other sponge and place this – sticky-side down – on top. Refrigerate overnight.

To serve, cut the trifle into squares or whatever shape you fancy, then coat with a spoonful of lightly whipped cream and drizzle across the melted chocolate.

# Cherry soup

FOR 6

This is served as a starter in Mittel Europa where soured cream, no wine and a lot less sugar are involved. I prefer it as a dessert with maybe a scoop of almond ice cream at its centre. The cherry season is short but the plums that follow will substitute nicely.

400g pitted red cherries

1 teaspoon plain flour

500ml rosé wine

1 cinnamon stick

1 vanilla pod – *split*

50g soft brown sugar

1 tablespoon lemon juice

### To finish

Almond ice cream or crème fraîche

Toasted flaked almonds

Put the cherries, flour, wine, cinnamon stick, vanilla pod, sugar and 100ml water in a pan. Bring to the boil, then simmer gently for 15 minutes.

Keep back a few cherries as decoration, discard the cinnamon and vanilla, then liquidise in a blender.

Return the soup to the pan and bring to the boil. Skim, pass through a strainer, and leave to cool.

When cold, add the lemon juice until the sharpness and sweetness are in balance. As this is the temperature at which you will eat the soup, it's best to make any final adjustments at this stage rather than earlier.

Serve with the reserved cherries, a scoop of ice cream or spoon of crème fraîche and scatter with a few flaked almonds.

# Buttermilk puddings with cardamom and honey strawberries

This pudding is embarrassingly easy to make. It's not seriously different in its method to a pannacotta and just as with that confection the key is to be brave with gelatine. Too much will render a result like a tennis ball. If your judgement fails and the pud doesn't quite set in time then serve it in the ramekin in which it was made with the fruit scattered around it. Better that way than hard and bouncy. An ancient Austrian pastry cook who used to teach me had a useful word of wisdom on the subject generally: 'However it turns out, you must always say that is how you meant it to be.' His other gems included 'When it's brown it's cooked and when it's black it's fucked.'

FOR 4–6

· · · · · · · · · · · · · · · · · · · · · · · · · · · · · · · · · · · · · · · · · · · · · · · · · · · · · · · · · · · · · · · · ·

400ml double cream

250g caster sugar

1 vanilla pod – *split and the seeds scraped into the cream*

4 strips of orange peel

Juice of ½ lemon

3 leaves gelatine – *softened in water for 20 minutes*

600ml buttermilk

Strawberries

1 large punnet strawberries – *hulled then halved*

1 tablespoon caster sugar

1 teaspoonful *crushed* cardamom seeds

Juice of 1 orange

1 tablespoon clear honey

Measure 200ml of the double cream into a bowl and whip to soft peaks. Put the remainder in a pan with the sugar, vanilla pod and orange peel and bring to the boil.

Remove from the heat, then stir in the lemon juice and gelatine. Strain into a clean jug.

Put the buttermilk in a bowl then gradually whisk in the hot cream mixture. Leave to cool.

When cold, fold in the whipped cream. Spoon the mixture into ramekins or dariole moulds and refrigerate overnight.

Put the strawberries into a serving bowl. Warm the sugar, cardamom seeds, orange juice and honey in a small pan, then spoon over the fruit. Serve with the pudding.

# Pistachio and apricot tart

FOR 6–10

There are a couple of points to watch here. The pastry isn't baked blind so needs to be rolled as thinly as possible and then rested before the tart goes in the oven. Also, bake in the centre of a preheated oven and place the tart directly on the oven shelf rather than on a baking tray, otherwise the pastry won't be crisp.

I have always made this using imperial measures and as it works have kept these here. It's not difficult, just ask your parents.

1 x 11-inch tart tin lined with sweet pastry (see Bakewell Tart on page 158)

5oz shelled, unsalted pistachios – plus 1oz for decorating the tart

3oz blanched almonds

1½ ounces plain flour

8oz unsalted butter – *softened to room temperature*

8oz caster sugar

4 eggs

8 large fresh apricots – *halved and stoned*

Put the pistachios, almonds and flour in a food processor and whizz until the consistency of breadcrumbs.

Cream together the butter and sugar, then beat in three of the eggs, one at a time. Add the nut mixture, then stir in the final egg. You will have a sort of pistachio frangipane.

Fill the tart case with the nut mixture and smooth its surface with a knife or spatula. Refrigerate for 2 hours.

Preheat the oven to 175°C/fan 150°C/gas mark 3. Arrange the apricot halves, cut-side down, on top of the nut mixture, scatter across the remaining whole pistachios, and bake for 40 minutes.

Rest the tart for 20 minutes before lifting from the tin.

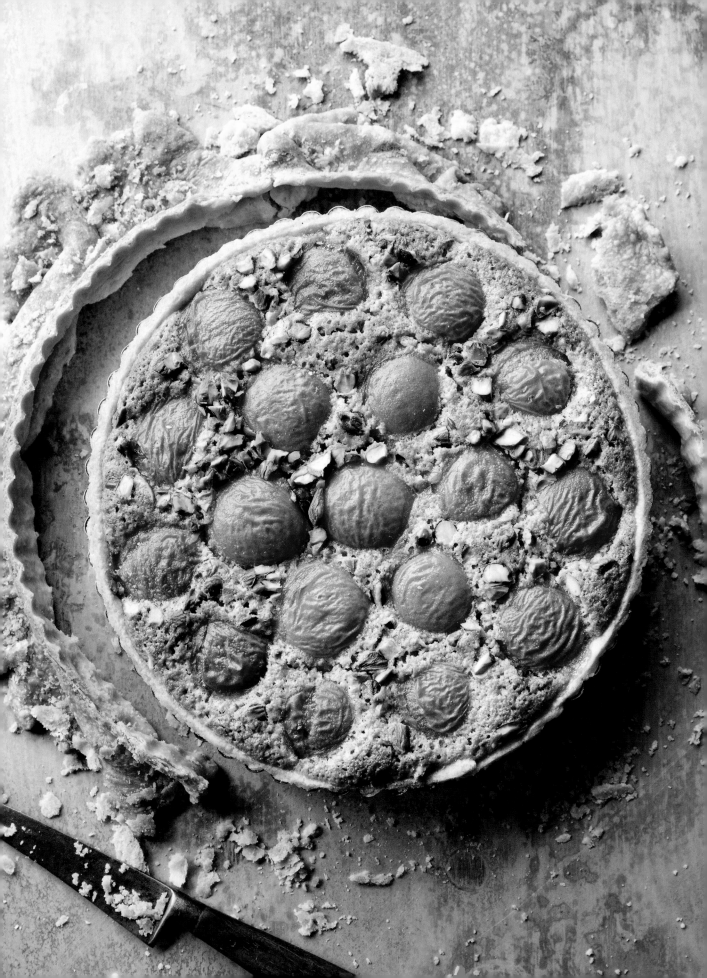

**9**

SOYA BEANS ARE
BEST LEFT FOR
CATTLE FEED

> My sardines might last you a century and your tomato purée would last me even longer.

The sort of items you keep in hand and their degree of antiquity will tell a lot about you. Sad tubs of largely unused Thai green curry mix or packs of ras el hanout that went out of date a year or so back highlight the adventures into cooking that didn't work for you. Jars of peaches in brandy or homemade chutneys and pickles that came as gifts and that you have forgotten to repackage and give to someone else.

The store cupboard is an opportunity to keep jars and tinned stuff, not just dry goods like spices and flour. Canning fruit and veg was another – not too distant – era's solution to seasonality and supply problems. Drying and fermenting must be the earliest, freezing and irradiation the latest. All (well, maybe not irradiation) have yielded fine products as accidental side effects of their preservation process.

What you keep will depend on what sort of things you cook and eat. So my sardines might last you a century and your tomato purée would last me even longer. Here are a few non-contentious ideas. I haven't included jams and preserves, as they are day-to-day ingredients, or anything that is best kept in the fridge once opened.

## FREEZERS AND FRIDGES

The store cupboard retains only a shadow of its previous significance. The main repository for food shopping we don't immediately need is either the fridge or the freezer. The fridge will be opened daily so won't be a place to quietly forget stuff you don't really want or need. As well as keeping your milk and white wine cold, it will showcase all your leftovers, pricking your conscience over waste and previous mealtime excess and overestimation.

There used to be a popular telly programme in which chefs were called upon to create a meal from a bag of unseen ingredients. Using these odds and ends is a similar challenge and you will feel particularly virtuous if you successfully empty the fridge and happily feed whoever eats in your house. Potato-based cakes – whether fish, corned beef or venison – are a well-tried option, but so are cromesquis and stuffed pancakes.

Freezers can be similar to store cupboards, preserving stuff best quietly binned. Most things will deteriorate in the freezer, just more slowly. Items not carefully wrapped or double wrapped will suffer freezer burn if stored badly or for too long. In restaurants, we are constrained to label everything with the date of freezing and this is a good idea at home too. It's amazing how quickly you can forget what you froze and when.

On the booze front, freezers have their uses. White spirits such as eau de vie, gin and vodka are fine from the freezer. I like a gin and tonic but hate the customary bar offering that has room temperature gin and room temperature tonic plus a handful of soft ice cubes and a sliver of lemon or lime. The cubes will melt into the drink before you are two swallows along rendering a flat, dilute, lukewarm drink. Think of a smaller glass with frozen gin and refrigerator-chilled tonic. Better. The smart, boutique gins that currently are on the market for the price of a family car are really best used in Martinis or as a straight drink. Why pay twice as much for a smart spirit, laden with nuances of orange peel and coriander then top it up with something like tonic water which is basically lemonade?

## PULSES

I am uncertain over the relative merits of tinned versus dried. Tinned chickpeas are a lot quicker of course because no overnight soaking is needed. And tinned petits pois are a completely different product from marrowfat or processed peas – neither of which are pleasant – and one I find completely delightful if handled properly. Different from fresh or frozen but equally fine if reheated with a little unsalted butter, lettuce and bacon as petits pois à la française.

Dried foods, like frozen, suffer from the misconception that they will last forever. So don't leave the chickpeas in the store cupboard indefinitely and if they have been hanging around for years, then be prepared to soak and boil them for longer than usual.

Small pulses like lentils won't really need soaking. It's the larger specimens, dried haricot beans, broad beans and the like, that should be left for long periods in water, overnight preferably, then boiled until quite soft in unsalted water (salt makes them tough).

Soya beans go down well in the Far East, but otherwise are best left for cattle feed. The artful Japanese turn this protein-crammed pulse into all sorts – tofu and miso paste mainly. Soy sauce is the finest use of these beans, mixed with malted wheat kernels and yeast, then blended with brine and fermented. The resulting brew, which takes months to mature, forms glutamates that enhance other food. That's the naturally brewed process of course and costs comparatively more. Nasty, non-brewed stuff that uses hydrochloric acid, corn syrup and colouring is also available, but why would you?

## TINNED FISH

Anchovies are essential: the brown jobs in olive oil rather than the silvery ones that you might eat on tapas or in a salad. Forget the fact that these are fish for they define meat dishes like steak tartare and, skewered into a leg, shoulder or rump of lamb will impart a savoury depth where you least expect.

 Sardines will mash into a respectable sandwich filling as will that strange tinned salmon popular after the war when little else was on offer and salmon was still considered a bit of a luxury. Tuna, though, is really good for sandwiches when mixed with plenty of mayonnaise, plenty of chopped spring onion and plenty of black pepper. The posher, and dearer, versions like belly tuna (ventresca) or yellowfin in olive oil are good for salade niçoise – a salad mixed with tomatoes, olives, boiled eggs and anchovies. I prefer this grade of tinned or jarred tuna for summer salads to the fresh fish. Seared fresh tuna is best considered as a completely separate ingredient, better for almost everything, except of course sandwiches and salade niçoise.

## MUSTARD

Most mustard is sold ready to eat rather than in powder form. English mustard is the strongest, Dijon and French are more aromatic than pungent, and German and Swedish mustards are mild, sometimes almost sweet. My preference is for the wholegrain Dijon stuff because it makes great mayonnaise, salad dressings and sauces. My father used to position a wedge of English mustard, which he made up himself, at the side of the plate, almost irrespective of what was being eaten. He told me many times how Colman's fortune had been made not just by the quantity of his mustard consumed but by the amount wasted by being left on the plate. Not sure what the moral of the story was but I'm sure he was right. I always thought it to be rather like mint sauce and redcurrant jelly, strong, bullying and a relic of a time when food was coarse and fatty.

# SAUCES AND RELISH

I have the relics of past, seemingly good ideas, in my fridge, such as hoisin and plum sauce, but only two items move through seamlessly from purchase to replacement: Tabasco and Worcestershire sauce.

Tabasco used to come in one colour – red – and strength – hot but not silly – but now comes in several. My taste buds are not thrilled by the searingly hot stuff, habanero for instance, which imparts nothing other than dynamite strength. The green, jalapeño, version which is comparatively milder contains no tabasco peppers and lends a fresh, almost citric, quality that I like. And I can always add a few more shakes of the bottle if I need extra heat or am making Bloody Marys. Tabasco, like good soy sauce, is a quality product. The McIlhenny company make it on Avery Island in Louisiana, near New Orleans. The peppers are mashed, salted, then fermented in oak barrels for three years. The result is mixed with vinegar, then aged some more before bottling. Tabasco keeps for years provided it isn't left in direct sunlight. I use it, in moderation, to balance creamy sauces or oily dressings and a touch in soup, like a drop of good vinegar or a squeeze of lemon, will freshen up the flavour.

Worcestershire sauce is mostly made in the Lea & Perrins factory in Worcester in the West Midlands. It's a happy legacy of the British Raj in India. The recipe is meant to be secret but it's a fermented concoction of Indian spices like tamarind with small fish similar to anchovies that is aged and matured before bottling. It is in some ways like the Thai and Vietnamese fish sauces, nam pla and nuoc mam, and has a lot in common with the first known sauce in the Mediterranean, garum. Garum was mentioned in tablets found in Egypt that pre-date the arrival of olives and olive oil. Fortunes were made by those who produced top-class garum and in the ruins of Pompeii there figured a shop selling the stuff that was part of a successful chain. The Romans, and ourselves while under their influence, used it as an all-purpose dip and particularly liked the salty tang such brews contain.

# Cromesquis

FOR 4

This is a device for leftovers that seems to have fallen into disuse amongst all the hash and burgers. It's a Polish or Russian dish in origin that was popular in France, especially amongst chefs who liked to maximise the possibilities of comparatively expensive ingredients. The idea is to make a small amount of thick white sauce, flavour it with herbs, mustard or whatever seems appropriate, then add bits of chopped chicken, ham or perhaps rabbit, along with maybe some boiled chopped leeks and onion. Leave to cool and solidify to the point it can be shaped into croquettes – a piping bag with no nozzle does the trick. The results are dipped in beaten egg then rolled in breadcrumbs and fried. Very nice with some salad and a sharp dressing. The ingredients here are a guideline, so cooked pork or veal would substitute for the chicken, as would ox tongue or some smoked sausage like Morteau or Montbéliard for the ham.

White sauce is as easy to make as to reconstitute from a packet. Traditionally, equal amounts of flour to butter were used for the roux. It's not only much easier to make and cook the roux if you use more butter, the result tastes better as well.

· · · · · · · · · · · · · · · · · · · · · · · · · · · · · · · · · · · · · · · · · · · · · · · · · · · · · · · · · · · · ·

50g butter

30g plain flour

100ml milk

250g cooked chicken and ham – *cut into dice*

1 tablespoon Dijon mustard

A little nutmeg

1 egg – *beaten*

100g white breadcrumbs or panko

Vegetable oil *for frying*

Salt and freshly ground black pepper

Make a roux by melting the butter then stirring in the flour. Let this cook a few moments before adding half the milk. Stir over a moderate heat until thick, almost solid, then stir in the remaining milk.

Stir in the diced chicken and ham, mustard and seasonings, then leave to cool and set.

Form patties or croquettes with the cooled mixture. Dip these in the beaten egg, then roll in the breadcrumbs.

Deep-fry in oil heated to 180°C, or shallow fry, until golden and crisp, also hot right the way through, then transfer to a warm oven for a few minutes.

Serve with tartare sauce or ketchup.

# Welsh rarebit

FOR 4

For a while I acted as consultant to the grand Piccadilly food store, Fortnum & Mason. They were immensely courteous and charming people and employed lots of experts on things like honey and marmalade. It was (and is still) the grocers of choice to royalty as well as the nouveaux riches and despite the obvious difference between my own unruly and untidy presence and their own tail coats and good manners, I rather enjoyed the experience. The chief executive even offered to sponsor me for membership of the East India Club in St James Square, which would have been a joke too far for a person brought up not far from Camden Town. Their speciality was welsh rarebit and they sold about a quarter of a million pounds worth of the snack each year. The recipe is simple but the secret of their success lay in avoiding any shortcuts on ingredient quality. The Cheddar has to be strong and well flavoured – Barbers, Keens or Montgomery, perhaps. The best bread is a white sourdough because this has the texture to withstand the cheese mixture without becoming flabby or soft while awaiting its turn under the grill.

350g strong top-quality Cheddar

20ml double cream

1 egg

35ml mustard – English or French, as you prefer

15ml Guinness or Murphy's stout

8 medium-sized slices of sourdough – *toasted*

Grate the cheese then stir together with the cream, egg, mustard and stout.

Spread on the toast, then grill until bubbling with patches of dark brown and yellow.

# Olive, tomato and parsley salad on toasted ciabatta or with linguine

FOR 6

This combination of every Italian ingredient you ever really liked makes a great salad. I have used it on toasted ciabatta alongside Parma ham and top-class salami in order to transform what is basically something bought from a good deli into a creditable lunch or first course. The same mixture can be stirred into al dente pasta, and thin linguine seem to work better than big fusilli, to make a good lunch. Green olives are fine pitted, or with anchovy or red pepper stuffing, but black olives aren't. This means you will have to cut the olive around the stone, which isn't quite as easy but scarcely qualifies as difficult. I prefer pecorino cheese to Parmesan in this dish but it may stretch the imagination to assume you have leftover pecorino rather than the more all-purpose Parmesan.

............

5 large tomatoes

2 tablespoons extra virgin olive oil – plus extra if serving with linguine

Zest of ¼ lemon

1 garlic clove – *crushed*

50g green olives – *stoned*

50g black olives – *stoned*

1 teaspoon capers

2 tablespoons *coarsely grated or shaved* Parmesan

2 heaped tablespoons *coarsely chopped* flat-leaf parsley

Freshly ground black pepper and green Tabasco sauce

Ciabatta loaf – *sliced* – or 500g linguine

Peel the tomatoes. If they are really firm you can do this with a sharp knife, but the general practice is to prick the tops and tails of each, then drop the tomatoes into boiling water, count to ten then refresh them in cold water. The skins will fall off. Halve the tomatoes, then scoop out the watery insides and seeds. Cut the remaining flesh into small dice.

Mix together the olive oil, lemon zest and garlic in a small bowl.

Cut all the olives into small dice and stir into the olive oil. Add the capers, tomatoes, Parmesan and parsley, then season with plenty of black pepper and a few drops of Tabasco.

Toast the ciabatta and then heap the salad on top.

Alternatively, boil the linguini in plenty of salted water until al dente, drain, season with salt and a little more olive oil then stir in the salad.

Shaved Parmesan just means you have used a vegetable peeler rather than a grater to produce larger but still thin results – it looks better but tastes the same.

# DRIED PASTA

Dried pasta is a store cupboard item whereas fresh pasta is a job of work. They are both delightful but in slightly different ways. Dried pasta comes in every conceivable size and shape. Italians say, and they should know, that each shape dramatically alters the finished dish even though the pasta ingredient proportions are identical. Evidently, the amount of sauce captured by any shape will change the nature of the dish. The main difference between pasta as eaten in Italy and pasta as eaten elsewhere, as far as I can see, is that Italians like more pasta and less sauce. The rest of us, the reverse.

> Hot steaming pasta will deliver a blast of heat to whatever is tossed into it.

When I was a child, pasta seemed to arrive in blue paper packaging as an immensely tall version of spaghetti. I never saw different shapes other than the truncated macaroni used for mac and cheese. Italians aren't the only noodle eaters, of course, so my childhood also saw my personal favourite, Vesta Chow Mein. This was a complex set of soft and crisp noodles plus various sachets of sauce. It was awkward to make and involved several frying pans. I look back on it with a mixture of nostalgia and horror, and am pleased to leave it in the memory rather than recreate it.

Uncooked as well as cooked sauces work well with pasta because the hot steaming pasta will deliver a blast of heat to whatever is tossed into it. In summertime, 500g of ripe tomatoes cut into cubes then macerated with crushed garlic, chillies and basil leaves, tossed in hot spaghetti then topped with some grated pecorino or Parmesan will be summer in a bowl.

Similarly, every variation on pesto will be a joy. Try a handful of pistachios as well as pine kernels in the pesto mixture for a change. This Sicilian version of pesto will taste fresh and vibrant. Use what shape you want and cook the pasta for whatever time it says on the packet. Al dente, slightly underdone, is always the most effective but beware, for raw pasta is no more thrilling than overcooked.

Italians regularly stipulate lots of salt in the water in which pasta is boiled. I think that the reason and effect is this: when the pasta is drained there will be an even coating of the cooking water across it. If this has been well salted then so will the pasta but in a completely even manner, everywhere that's wet being similarly coated with salt. It's often said that a little olive oil in the water helps separate the pasta strands. Not sure but never taken any chances.

# CHEESE

Cheese seems the perfect fast food. As with charcuterie, the work is done by others who are skilled, and you should have ready-made food that isn't junk. It's a matter of clever shopping and careful storage. You can make rudimentary cheeses yourself – fresh goat's cheese maybe – by warming the milk with rennet then straining the curds that form from the whey. It's a bit more complex, of course, if you want the cheese to taste of anything individual. The salting, adding of specific bacteria, pressing and moulding will determine the smell and character of the cheese.

As important as the manufacture of cheese is the ripening, the bringing into perfect condition, what the French call 'affinage'. If you have bought a Brie that is chalky at the centre, then you have bought something inferior that will be very difficult to put right. Neither you nor I will have the controlled conditions necessary to ripen the cheese properly. The outside will soften and run before the centre ripens. Only buy cheeses that are ready to eat. It's a skill to bring the cheese into prime condition and even top supermarkets haven't mastered it. Most big stores will promote hard cheeses that are less prone to over-ripening or industrial cheeses designed to be kept refrigerated.

# Burrata with summer vegetable salad and chickpea fritters

Burrata is the smarter, creamier version of mozzarella, well the more expensive version anyway, and a bit luxurious. The texture is that of a firmly poached egg and it can truly be said to offer a summer treat. The inevitable tomato and basil accompaniment will work fine here, as it does with mozzarella, but this is also good and the hot crisp fritters give a contrast of both texture and temperature.

FOR 4

· · · · · · ·· · · ● ● ● ·● · · ● · ·● · ·● · ·● · · · · · · · · · · ·● · · · ● · · · · · ●● · · · ● · · · ●● · ·● · · · · · · · ·● ● · · · · · · · ● ● · · · ·· ·

200g burrata

### Salad

100g peas – *fresh or frozen*

2 baby artichokes – *thinly sliced*

100g broad beans, *peeled*

Zest and juice of ½ lemon – *macerated together*

A few basil leaves – *torn*

1 tablespoon olive oil

4 radishes – *thinly sliced*

A few watercress leaves

### Fritters

250g chickpea (gram) flour

Salt and freshly ground black pepper

A large bunch of flat-leaf parsley – *coarsely chopped*

Oil *for deep-frying*

½ lemon

Blanch the peas, artichokes and broad beans. This means dropping them into boiling salted water then draining while still fairly crisp and refreshing under cold running water. This preserves both the colour and texture.

Mix the lemon, basil and oil, then toss the blanched vegetables in this dressing along with the radishes and watercress leaves.

To make the fritters, stir together the flour and 75ml cold water and season with salt and pepper. Pour into a saucepan and whisk over a moderate heat until thick. Continue to simmer, stirring occasionally, for 5 minutes, then stir in the parsley and remove from the heat.

Turn the mixture onto oiled greaseproof or nonstick paper and spread to a thickness of 5mm with a flat-bladed or palette knife. When cooled, cut into diamond shapes.

Heat the oil and deep-fry the fritters, in batches, until crisp. Drain on kitchen paper and season with salt and a few drops of lemon juice.

Serve 50g burrata per person on cold plates with a small heap of the vegetable salad to one side and some hot fritters.

# Pasta with Sicilian almond and mint pesto

FOR 4

Sicily has a longer food heritage than Italy. In the classical period, the island was very rich, and spoke Greek rather than Latin. The patricians in Rome would have wanted a Sicilian cook in much the same way as Edwardian aristocracy here wanted a Frenchman. The Normans ran Sicily in the Middle Ages and the access to its spicing and kitchen skill made Norman, then English, cookery the most sophisticated in Europe. For a while anyway. It's still distinctive and delicious.

4 tablespoons olive oil

2 garlic cloves – *crushed*

250g cherry tomatoes – *cut into quarters*

1 small red chilli – *chopped*

1 bunch of basil leaves – *chopped*

100g almonds – *toasted*

1 teaspoon capers

1 tablespoon mint leaves – *chopped*

400g dried pasta

Salt

Heat half the oil in a pan, then fry the garlic, tomatoes and chilli. Gently stew for 5 minutes then transfer to a large bowl.

Blend the basil, almonds, capers and mint with the remaining olive oil and some salt. You can struggle with a mortar and pestle or press the button on a spice grinder or food processor.

Cook the pasta until al dente, drain, then toss with the tomato, garlic and oil.

Stir in the mint and almond pesto and serve.

# Risotto bianco

FOR 4

My personal preference is for a risotto flavoured with herbs, mushrooms or vegetables rather than a lump of meat or fish, both of which relegate the rice to bit-part player in the meal. The textures and the interplay between cheese, stock, wine and rice are good enough – more than good enough.

1 tablespoon olive oil

1 tablespoon *chopped* onion

150g vialone or carnaroli rice

100ml white wine

500ml warm chicken or vegetable stock – *take care if you use the little pots or cubes as they are salty*

50g unsalted butter

50g grated Parmesan

Salt and freshly ground black pepper

Heat the oil in a large, heavy-based casserole and fry the onion then the rice. The rice needs the burst of heat before any liquid is added.

Season with salt and pepper, add the wine, then let it reduce away completely.

Stir in half the stock. Bring to the boil, then cover with a lid and remove from the heat. The rice will absorb all the stock but remain hard and partially cooked. At this point you can turn off the heat and keep the risotto until 10 minutes before you are ready to eat. It won't suffer and won't cook further.

Add the remaining stock and bring back to the boil. Simmer until most, but not all, of the liquid has been absorbed.

Stir in the butter then the Parmesan, then anything else you want to add to the dish.

## RISOTTO

Success with risotto involves a combination of heat and liquid, and the proportions are as time dependent as any soufflé. It used to be the case that a sadly overcooked risotto would appear, but now a bowlful of grit is the more likely option. Rice will continue to cook by absorbing hot liquid, so removing the pan from the heat doesn't help if there is still stock or water to continue swelling the rice. A good risotto will have some resistance or bite in its grains but will still be a soft and gloopy dish. You see the problem. Left alone the rice will take in whatever liquid is there, overcooking in the process. You can halt this cooking by rationing the amount of stock and wine used. The good news is that the cooking can be restarted whenever you want by adding more liquid and heat and this is what restaurants, as well as canny home cooks, will do.

What piece of meat, mushroom or vegetable you decide on to set off the dish is subsidiary to cooking the risotto properly. I am fond of an early summer courgette and some peas with some basil or parsley, stirred in at the final moment, or porcini – fresh is fine, but dried then reconstituted and chopped up will do. The basics are the texture of the rice and its stock.

The rice varieties used come under the umbrella of arborio rice – Italian short grain rice. The great Arrigo Cipriani of Harry's Bar in Venice advocates vialone nano but others prefer the hybrid carnaroli. They are all rugby ball shaped grains that will give a firm finish.

# Blue cheese and sesame biscuits

MAKES 20 SMALL BISCUITS

These simple biscuits have been my favourite snack with drinks for years, so apologies if I have mentioned them before. I have made them slightly larger on occasion and squirted beetroot and horseradish purée on top so they look a little more posh and interesting. I've also served them alongside gravadlax and prosciutto for grand canapé situations. I'm sure you're not silly enough to cater for this sort of event but will enjoy them as they are. I try to use Roquefort or Stilton, but any blue cheese that isn't too soft – a mountain Gorgonzola or Bresse Bleu perhaps – will be just fine. A perfect use of leftover blue cheese in fact, better than the overpowering dressings you may have tried to use it for previously. The biscuits are crumbly, so vacuuming of carpet will be a factor next day. Serve them bite sized and warm.

100g unsalted butter – *cut into cubes*

100g self-raising flour

100g blue cheese – *crumbled*

50g sesame seeds

Use a food processor to blend the butter and flour to the texture of breadcrumbs. Add the cheese and process for a further few seconds, on the pulse setting. You don't want a blue purée.

Turn out and knead the mixture a couple of times to evenly distribute all the ingredients, then refrigerate until needed. Chill briefly before cooking if you have time.

Preheat the oven to 180°C/fan 160°C/gas mark 4.

Scoop or pinch out small pieces of the dough and roll these into balls about 2.5cm across. Toss these in the sesame seeds.

Space the balls out on a baking tray and then bake for about 10 minutes or until firm and golden.

# Smoked eel and brandade with light horseradish cream

FOR 4

Here again, the idea of leftovers lying at the corner of the fridge is not possible in my household as smoked eel is a favourite, also too expensive to be forgotten about. I have altered this dish as far as restaurant use is concerned. The estimable chef, Jeremy Lee, at Quo Vadis in Soho, used to offer a smoked eel sandwich as a starter, and I have to say I really liked it. So now I put the brandade between two slices of sourdough and toast it rather than spoon it next to the fillets. There are three fairly simple components to the dish. First the smoked eel itself, which I buy from either Brown & Forrest Smokery in Somerset or Forman's in London. All the tail bits and trimmings go into the brandade, then a dollop of horseradish cream as accompaniment. Brandade is the name of a dish of salt cod and olive oil served in the south of France and Spain. If you don't fancy using eel, the same idea works well with smoked mackerel, and in this case I would buy the fish, by post, from the great Frank Hederman in County Cork, more expensive than, the supermarket but worlds apart from the usual offerings.

I prefer to make the horseradish cream from fresh horseradish rather than use a jar. It's actually quite easy – all you need do is peel the root, wrap it in clingfilm, then freeze it. You can grate the horseradish from frozen or even shave it like Parmesan.

---

200g smoked eel fillets

### Horseradish cream

200ml double cream

1 teaspoon Dijon mustard

1 tablespoon fresh horseradish

A few drops of lemon juice

### Brandade

100g smoked eel fillet

1 teaspoon Dijon mustard

1 teaspoon horseradish cream

2 tablespoons olive oil

150ml double cream

1 teaspoon lemon juice

A few drops of Tabasco sauce

First make the horseradish cream. Whip the double cream with the mustard, fresh horseradish and lemon juice until thick.

To make the brandade, chop the smoked eel and combine with the rest of the ingredients to make a rillettes-like paste.

Lay slices of the smoked eel fillets on plates with a spoonful of brandade plus a spoonful of horseradish cream.

# Chicken liver tart

FOR 4

Quiches have a serious image problem, largely the result of crap winebars offering dishes containing little egg, no cream and rubbish pastry alongside nasty ham and cheese, battery chicken in some herbal disguise and mysterious 'Mediterranean' vegetables. Real quiche is a real treat. At Carrier's we used to offer a miniature one as a second course with maybe spinach and ricotta or shrimps, bacon and parsley as filling. This recipe wasn't one we ever offered but is my favourite. The taste is rather like a chicken liver pâté only lighter, more delicate and of course warm. I've included a recipe for the pastry but you could of course buy ready made.

The main pitfall could be the appearance. Light brown stuff has no visual appeal and will need help. Three or four minutes under a hot grill or – if you have such a thing – a blasting with a blow torch will transform the look to one of golden attraction rather than cow pat.

### Pastry

1 egg, plus a little beaten egg, *for eggwash*

260g unsalted butter – *softened*

250g plain flour

½ teaspoon salt

1 tablespoon milk

### Filling

150g *trimmed* chicken livers

2 garlic cloves – *chopped*

1 shallot – *chopped*

1 tablespoon brandy

3 eggs

250ml double cream

1 tablespoon *shredded* basil leaves

A little *grated* nutmeg

Salt and freshly ground black pepper

First make the pastry case. Stir the egg and butter together, then work in the flour and salt. Add the milk, then knead a few times to be sure that all is well mixed. Rest the pastry in the fridge for 1–2 hours.

Preheat the oven to 200°C/fan 180°C/gas mark 6.

Roll out the pastry to line a 26cm tart tin, preferably one with a detachable base. Brush with beaten egg then bake blind for 10 minutes. Remove from the oven. If the pastry has bubbled up, use a cloth to gently press it back into place. Reduce the temperature to 150°C/fan 130°C/gas mark 2.

Make the filling by puréeing the chicken livers, garlic, shallot and brandy in a liquidiser. Add the eggs and cream then briefly blend once more. Finally add the basil leaves and seasonings, blend and taste.

Pour the filling into the tart case and bake in the centre of the oven for about 30 minutes until firm and set. Leave for a few minutes before unmoulding.

Serve with a green salad in walnut dressing.

# KEEP BUGGERING ON

The Merchant House was a restaurant in Ludlow that my wife, Anja, and I ran for 11 years. I cooked alone most of the time. It was successful, turned in a modest profit and kept us independent of corporate types in suits. We loved it, we liked most of the people who came to eat and we thought the little medieval town a complete delight. But 11 years is quite long enough in the same format and it was time to close up before getting stale.

When we closed the doors for the final service the intention was for me to earn a living pontificating on food matters, writing recipe columns and acting as consultant to the odd hotel or restaurant. This was a sound plan. The money is good, one's reputation is untouchable – there being no restaurant in operation to destroy it – and there was the possibility of having weekends and evenings free for the first time in 40 years.

So when one of my favourite restaurants, The Walnut Tree, went into receivership I wasn't tempted. It had endured a sad few years and was about ready for quiet euthanasia. Its glory days had been under the ownership of Franco Taruschio and his wife Ann, who ran the place for 38 years. They nursed it from rural pub to national institution with a blend of Welsh ingredients and Italian flare. The dishes became almost legendary. Vincisgrassi, a sort of lasagne with porcini and Parma ham, or brodetto, a vast fish stew, were typical. When the Taruschios sold up, vast numbers of The Walnut Tree's fans and followers went into mourning for a lost institution. Myself included.

> When the Taruschios sold up, vast numbers of The Walnut Tree's fans and followers went into mourning for a lost institution. Myself included.

The brave duo who took on this revered spot were top London chef, Stephen Terry, and restaurant manager Francesco Matteoli. Initially all went well. The food was different, still Italian, but still spectacularly good. A Michelin star and good reviews followed. But so, too, did arguments between the two partners. Stephen Terry left and a series of chefs took charge, none of whom managed to return the kitchen to its former glory. Then came the worst decision, to participate in Gordon Ramsay's *Kitchen Nightmares*. The idea of the programme is that Ramsay sees a failing business, advises on what's being done wrong, then oversees the corrective treatment. Along the way though, Francesco was portrayed as arrogant and greedy, charging vast sums and failing to deliver the goods on the plate. Whatever the rights and wrongs, the programme was catastrophic for the restaurant and remains, even now, as the only thing for which the place is regularly remembered (today's email has two messages from the part of the US where it is currently being shown). Business dwindled and eventually the bank called in its loans.

I thought to resuscitate the place. A chap who had worked with me at Merchant House offered a 50/50 partnership, which would halve the risk, and to look after things like maintenance and bureaucracy from his nearby hotel if I ran the restaurant. Seemed a fair proposition, so I agreed. The place had been closed for the best part of a year, was in poor structural condition and had never been other than a top-end Italian restaurant. It was a nuisance that the economy lurched into deep recession. This sort of thing doesn't usually affect me as much as others, as the core lunchtime trade in the provinces lies with grey haired persons like myself, who have – unlike myself – made provision for their retirement with savings and investments. Very low interest rates and poorly performing stock markets knock them hard. Anyway, so far so good.

The dishes that appear on the menu now are a reflection of taste combinations that I have enjoyed over the years. A brigade of cooks to help with the preparation and cooking of the food extends the range of dishes possible. Running a restaurant is almost addictive. The initial idea of setting things up with a skilled chef, decent brigade and waiting staff, then putting in the occasional appearance to check that all's well was fine in theory but not in practice – you have to pitch up and work rather than send encouraging memos. I did manage to find a top class chef, Roger Brook, to work with me who had not only worked with the Taruschios back in the day so knew how the place operated , but had once worked briefly with myself. He came with his wife Marta who is restaurant manager. Also the formidable Pauline, who has been at the place for over 40 years and knows everyone who has ever eaten there.

In common with large tracts of the rest of Britain, Wales sports some fabulous produce but not a vast cookery tradition. Like their Celtic cousins, the Irish and Scots, there is a history of treating simply what's available, though too much rain, Chapel and a comparative absence – until recently – of wine and beer make for food that is good for you rather than fun. My view is that this is largely good news. A clean slate unconstrained by a definite and unquestioned culinary tradition can free you to make the best of what's available now rather than what may have been on offer a hundred years ago. The real difference between nations is more a question of taste and climate. Working to these differences while using the finest produce is what matters, rather than making some slavish imitation of what's popular in Lyon or Palermo or, worse, pretending that there is a massive gastronomic heritage when there is not.

So it's fish and sheep then is it? Not necessarily. There are good ingredients across the country, artisan cheese makers, people who rear rare breed pigs, Welsh Black cattle and much more. And the cooking extends beyond Welsh cakes and laverbread. As it happens, I dislike the taste and texture of laverbread, a braised seaweed, so you will find no recipes for it here anyway. More importantly, there are people who come out to eat and enjoy themselves, even on weekdays when it's nobody's birthday. They are what keep us going.

> Using the finest produce is what matters, rather than making some slavish imitation of what's popular in Lyon or Palermo or, worse, pretending that there is a massive gastronomic heritage when there is not.

# Index

First published in Great Britain in 2016 by Kyle Books,
an imprint of Kyle Cathie Ltd

192–198 Vauxhall Bridge Road
London SW1V 1DX
general.enquiries@kylebooks.com

www.kylebooks.co.uk

10 9 8 7 6 5 4 3 2 1

ISBN 978 0 85783 338 9

Text © 2016 Shaun Hill
Design © 2016 Kyle Books
Photographs © 2016 Tamin Jones

Editor: Judith Hannam
Editorial Assistant: Hannah Coughlin
Copy Editor: Stephanie Evans
Designer: Anita Mangan
Photographer: Tamin Jones
Food Stylist: Annie Rigg
Prop Stylist: Liz Belton
Production: Nic Jones and Gemma John

A Cataloguing in Publication
record for this title is available
from the British Library.

Colour reproduction by f1 colour

Printed and bound in China by C&C Offset
Printing Co., Ltd.

I'd like to thank all at Kyle Books
for asking me to write this book
and especially to my editor,
Judith Hannam, whose advice was
usually sound and temperament
unfailingly positive. Also to Annie
Rigg, who cooked all this stuff for
the photography.

Recipes belong to no one and are
generally versions of traditional
food and flavour combinations
helped along by improvements in
availabilities and the occasional
inspirational idea. If I have failed
to credit anyone or any country's
heritage, then apologies.